AN INTRODUCTION
TO THE ARCHITECTURAL
HERITAGE *of*

DUBLIN
NORTH
CITY

Merlo Kelly

An Roinn
Ealaíon, Oidhreachta agus Gaeltachta
Department of
Arts, Heritage and the Gaeltacht

ORMOND QUAY LOWER

Foreword

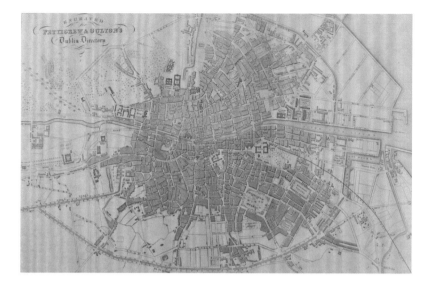

Dublin, Ireland's capital city, has a distinguished architectural legacy that stretches from the medieval period to the present. There are the large set-pieces, public buildings and public spaces, such as the Four Courts and Mountjoy Square, and the historic Liffey quays and bridges. However, most of the city's historic structures are domestic and commercial, and many of them are barely noticed. The canals and railways, which frame the north city, have provided vital infrastructure, but also leave their own legacy of historic structures. A significant aspect of the cityscape is the host of well-crafted details, ranging from integral parts of façades, such as fanlights and balconies, to boundaries formed by cast-iron railings and gates, and street furniture such as coal hole covers and post boxes.

This Introduction seeks to give a representative picture of the north city and its historic structures.

The Architectural Inventory of Dublin North City was carried out in phases in 2011-14. Over 2,800 structures were recorded. However, it should not be regarded as exhaustive as, over time, other buildings and structures of merit will come to light. The purpose of the Inventory and of this book is to explore the social and historical context of the buildings and their setting and to facilitate a greater appreciation of the built heritage of the city.

The NIAH survey of the architectural heritage of Dublin City can be accessed on the internet at: *www.buildingsofireland.ie*

NIAH NATIONAL INVENTORY
of ARCHITECTURAL HERITAGE

Introduction

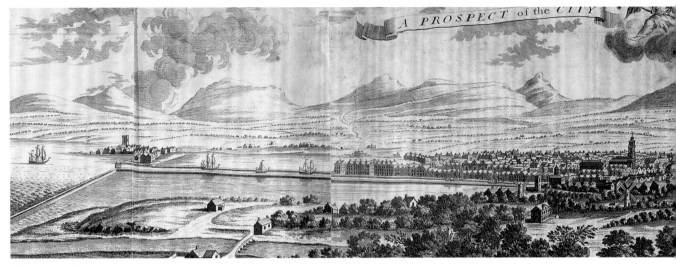

A MAP OF THE CITY
AND SUBURBS OF
DUBLIN by Charles
Brooking (1728)

*Courtesy of Royal Irish
Academy*

Dublin's topographical setting on the east coast, at the mouth of the river Liffey and sheltered by mountains to the south and southwest, has shaped its character as the capital city. The narrative of Dublin's layered history is manifest in its built heritage. The city's phased development hinges around the earliest Gaelic and Viking settlements, and its medieval core remains embedded in the urban form. Dublin North City is bounded by the Liffey to the south, the Royal Canal to the north and includes Phoenix Park to the west. The morphology of the district was largely defined by the lands of St Mary's Abbey and was shaped by developers in the seventeenth and eighteenth centuries. A series of land reclamation projects at the seaward end of the city facilitated an eastward expansion.

Dublin's status as a major city, the sixth largest in Europe in the eighteenth century, is clearly reflected in the magnificence of the architecture dating from this period. Unadorned red brick terraces formed the elegant streets and squares, creating a backdrop for stately public buildings and palatial town houses, these latter typically expressed in granite, limestone and Portland stone *(fig. 1)*. The culture of the developer, which began in the late seventeenth century, contributed to a re-working of the historic urban form. The ideologies of the European Enlightenment permeated Irish culture, influencing literary, artistic and architectural endeavours. Much of the inherited cityscape belongs to this era, a time of pivotal growth and visionary thinking in terms of urban design, which saw the consolidation of the Jervis and Gardiner estates north of the river.

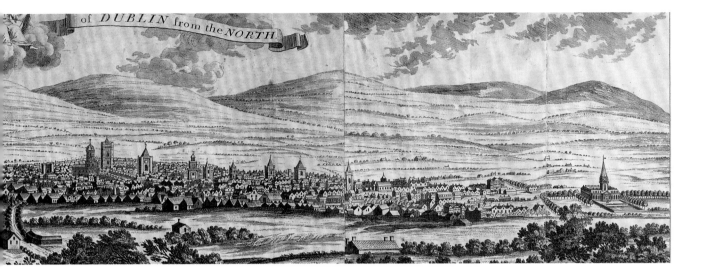

of DUBLIN from the NORTH

(fig. 1)
LOWER GARDINER
STREET
(c.1825)

(Fig. 2)
CHURCH OF ST FRANCIS XAVIER
Dominick Street
Upper
(1832)

St Francis Xavier's dramatic classical interior is dominated by the sumptuous reredos.

The establishment of the Wide Streets Commission in 1757 created a body with an overview of planning and design within the city. With their increased powers over developments in private estates, the Commissioners were poised to oversee and implement urban improvement on a grand scale. By the close of the century, a pattern of routes, civic spaces and composed vistas had become imprinted on the north city, interwoven with the medieval road pattern.

The early nineteenth century was marked by a surge in church building, which intensified after Catholic Emancipation in 1829 *(fig. 2)*. Rising levels of poverty and a lack of adequate housing resulted in appalling slum conditions as the century progressed, with many Georgian town houses falling into tenements. Social issues began to drive the building programme, resulting in the construction of housing, hospitals and prisons. The completion of the Royal Canal and the arrival of the railway facilitated new levels of trade and commerce, accompanied by an economic boom that led to the establishment of many new commercial premises across the city. Ornate façades and shopfronts decorated the earlier buildings that were commonly adapted to house these new businesses.

The twentieth century was a time of upheaval, defined in its opening decades by an ongoing housing crisis and by the civil unrest that accompanied the movement for national independence. The north city, ravaged by the turbulence of the period, was the subject of an ambitious reconstruction project undertaken in the 1920s *(fig. 3)*. Despite significant infrastructural change, Dublin remained a relatively compact city at the start of the century, but the demand for housing led to the creation of expansive suburbs in the 1930s and 1940s, in addition to city centre housing schemes *(fig. 4)*. Economic prosperity in the 1960s inspired new confidence as Modernist influences from the United States and Continental Europe permeated the Irish architectural scene. This phase was accompanied by slum clearances, leading to the destruction of swathes of Georgian fabric. Prompted by a re-evaluation of civic development, Dublin experienced what has been referred to as an 'urban renaissance' in the closing decades of the twentieth century, where an emphasis was placed on urban regeneration and considerable investment was made in the conservation of historic structures.

(Fig. 3)
18-19 HENRY STREET
(1917)

The date plaque testifies to the rebuilding of much of the O'Connell Street area in the wake of the Easter Rising. The façade displays good craftsmanship in brick and stone.

(Fig. 4)
CHANCERY HOUSE
Chancery
Place/Charles Street
West
(1934-5)

Herbert Simms, City Housing Architect, designed this housing block, fronted by a small park with arched gateways and a kiosk. It stands across the street from the side of the Four Courts.

Pre 1700

DUBLIN (1610)

St Michan's Church, St Mary's Abbey and St Saviour's Priory are all depicted on John Speed's map of Dublin, which presents a portrait of the medieval city on the brink of a rich phase of expansion.

Courtesy of Royal Irish Academy

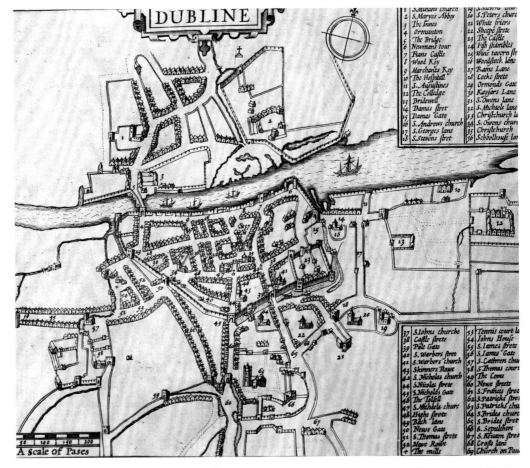

Viking settlers established *Dyfflin* in 841 on the south bank of the river Liffey, having travelled from the Norwegian fjords as raiders. The settlement was strategically placed at *Áth Cliath* (Irish, 'ford of wattle-work'), a historic crossing point at the confluence of the Liffey and Poddle rivers, and a nucleus of ancient routes across Ireland. The location presented natural advantages: a sheltered port with the opportunity for sea trade and a network of river connections providing natural harbours.

The Hiberno-Norse period (c. 980-1170) saw the emergence of settlement north of the river in Oxmantown Wood. St Michan's Church and St Mary's Abbey date from this time. These two religious houses acted as generators of urban

(Fig. 5)

**ST MICHAN'S
CHURCH**
Church Street
(1685)

A church was founded
here in 1095 by the
Hiberno-Norse. The
present building dates
from 1686 and was
renovated in 1825.
The tower and stair
turret have rubble
calp limestone walls,
with cut stone to the
ground floor. St
Michan's was an early
medieval ecclesiastical
site, its round
enclosure being
identified in
archaeological
excavations.

form, affirming the arrangement of ancient thoroughfares converging on the urban core to the south. St Michan's was founded in 1095 on the site of an early monastery and was a focal point of this transpontine community *(fig. 5)*. It is situated on Church Street, one of the *slighte* (ancient highways of Ireland), a northern route from the pre-Norse Áth Cliath and around which the northern suburb evolved. St Mary's Abbey, initiated as a Savigniac (reformed Benedictine order) house in 1139, commanded considerable lands to the east. In 1147, the abbey adopted the Cistercian rule, constituting the order's wealthiest Irish monastery in an atypical, urban rather than rural, setting.

Following the capture of Dublin by the Anglo-Normans in 1170, the remaining Hiberno-Norse population was displaced to the northern suburb of Oxmantown. English influences pervaded building practices in the walled city as King John set about consolidating a defensive capital. He ordered the construction of a royal castle (Dublin Castle) in 1204 and strengthened and extended the Hiberno-Norse fortifications, facilitated by major land reclamation at Wood Quay.

With land in Dublin and further afield amounting to almost 6,000 acres, St Mary's Abbey was a pivotal centre of power and influence until the Dissolution of the Monasteries in the mid-sixteenth century. Its chapter house functioned as a meeting place for the Parliament and Privy Council, and an occasional home for the Viceroy. The abbey was well served with extensive fishing rights

(Fig. 6)
ST MARY'S ABBEY
Meetinghouse Lane
(1139, rebuilt early
14th century)

St Mary's Abbey was
founded as a
Benedictine monastery
in 1139 and became
a Cistercian house in
1147. It was
supressed by Henry
VIII in 1539.

Image from Dublin,
One Thousand Years
by Stephen Conlin,
The O'Brien Press Ltd.

The chapter house dates
from about 1200 and
displays the earliest rib vault
in an Irish Cistercian
building. Fragments of the
cloister arcade are displayed
within.

*Courtesy of the Photographic
Unit, DAHG*

(Fig. 7)
**FATHER MATHEW
BRIDGE**
(1816-18)

Father Mathew Bridge
connects Bridge Street
and Church Street in
the medieval core of
Dublin. It was built
on the site of a series
of earlier bridges,
known as 'Dublin
Bridge' or 'Old
Bridge', the earliest of
timber and which was
replaced with a stone
bridge in about 1210.
The bridge stands just
to the east of the
original Áth Cliath
(ford of wattlework).

and a harbour on the Liffey, a fleet of trading ships and a marketplace to the west, on the site of today's City Fruit & Vegetable Market. A network of roads and associated urban spaces emanated from the abbey, the boundaries of which defined the form of the early north city. Constructed predominantly of timber, the abbey was destroyed by the great Oxmantown fire of 1304 and was substantially rebuilt in masonry. Today only the chapter house, dating from about 1200, and an adjoining slype or passageway, survives, hidden within a nineteenth-century warehouse *(fig. 6)*. There was another abbey, the Dominican priory of St Saviour, built about 1218, at the location of the present Four Courts.

The first bridge over the Liffey, connecting the walled city to Oxmantown, was of timber. It was replaced in stone about 1210 and was known as Dublin Bridge or Old Bridge until the mid-nineteenth century. Today the fine three-arched Father Mathew Bridge stands on the site *(fig. 7)*.

THE CITY AND SUBURBS OF DUBLIN (1673)

Bernard de Gomme's map shows the development of the Smithfield area, with its bowling green of 1666, and the market place of Smithfield with ninety-nine lots, laid out around it to attract commercial and residential lessees.

Courtesy of National Maritime Museum, Greenwich

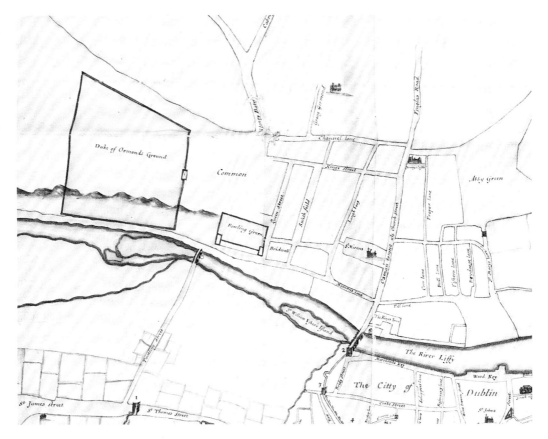

The arrival of the Black Death in 1348, and further epidemics in the fifteenth and sixteenth centuries, resulted in a prolonged period of stagnation. The portrait of the city in the early fifteenth century is that of a besieged and depopulated place, rife with disease, and its castle in ruins. The Dissolution of the Monasteries in 1539 resulted in the destruction of most religious houses and the plundering of their remains to repair Dublin Castle. A number of religious institutions, notably St Mary's Abbey and St Saviour's Priory, were acquired for state or private use. The latter became the site of the King's Inns in 1582, commencing a longstanding juridical presence on the north quays.

The population of the city increased from approximately 10,000 in 1610 to 75,000 in 1710, and this surge is reflected in the metamorphosis of the urban landscape. The concept of a formally designed streetscape emerges in this period, manifesting the aspiration to create a pleasant living environment for the burgeoning middle class. A phase of sophisticated suburban development marked the second half of the

(Fig. 8)
ASHTOWN CASTLE
Phoenix Park
(c.1605)

Ashtown Castle, dated to about 1605 by analysis of a section of roof timber found during the restoration, was incorporated into the Under Secretary's Lodge, the building later serving as the Papal Nunciature.

ASHTOWN CASTLE
Aerial view, showing the plan of the Papal Nunciature, demolished about 1980, represented by hedging.

Courtesy of the Photographic Unit, DAHG

seventeenth century, originating on the Aungier estate and progressing north of the river under the direction of the City Assembly and the Duke of Ormonde, then viceroy, who was to become highly influential in the development of the north city. The architectural historian Maurice Craig writes about Ormonde's arrival in 1662, a defining moment in the city's urban history: '...*James Duke of Ormonde stepped out of his pinnace on to the sands of Dublin Bay. The Renaissance, in a word, had arrived in Ireland.'*

In 1665, while plots were being laid out and leased around St Stephen's Green, to the south of the river, the City Assembly decreed that the lands of Oxmantown Green were to be similarly divided and let by lot, allowing the formation of a series of residential streets, a marketplace and a bowling green. Smithfield

Market, a spacious market place served by Queen Street and the adjoining Haymarket, is the most enduring legacy of this chapter of development in the north city. Both Oxmantown Green (or Common) and Smithfield feature on Bernard de Gomme's map of 1673 and Brooking's map of 1728.

While Ormonde's intentions of constructing a mansion for himself on lands annexed for his use to the west of Smithfield never materialised, he acquired the lands of St John's Priory at Kilmainham and created Phoenix Park in 1662. This enclosed royal deer-park was the largest of its kind in Europe, with vast parklands measuring 2,000 acres, until the lands of the Royal Hospital and Chapelizod were set apart. The park absorbed Ashtown Castle, an early seventeenth-century tower house *(fig. 8)*.

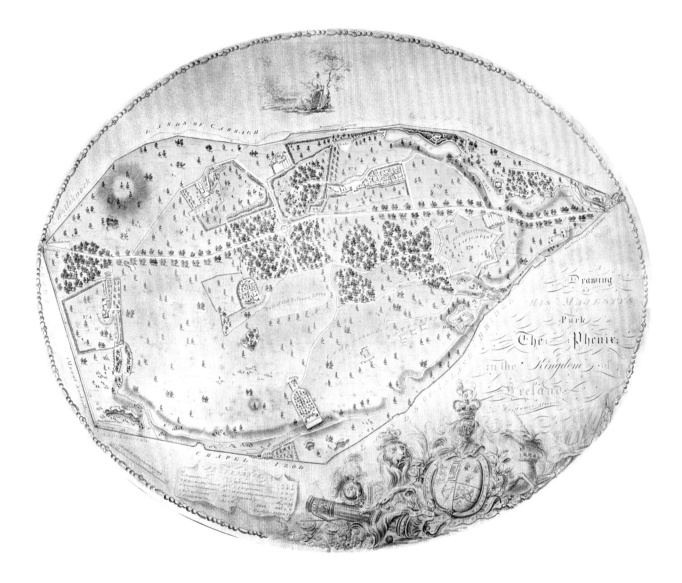

(Fig. 9)
**29 ORMOND QUAY
LOWER**
(c.1680)

This house dates to
the late seventeenth
century. It is a yellow
brick structure with a
pitched slate roof. It
displays a rusticated
rendered ground floor
and evidence of later
alterations.

**DRAWING OF HIS
MAJESTY'S PARK THE
PHENIX IN THE
KINGDOM OF
IRELAND**

Phoenix Park before
the early nineteenth-
century realignment
of roads. The formal
crossroads at the
Phoenix Monument,
with plantations to
the four quadrants, is
the strongest feature.
The Magazine Fort,
close to the south-
eastern edge, was
part of a broader
military use of the
park, indicated by the
'batteries' and
'targett' to its west.
'Lord Wharton's
Fortification' to the
northeast, designed
by Thomas Burgh and
underway in 1710,
was never completed.

*Courtesy of the
Embassy of the United
States of America*

Following the Great Fire of London in 1666, stringent building standards were introduced in urban centres in Britain and Ireland, prohibiting timber structures and prescribing masonry construction, slate or tiled roofs and flush façades. The influence of these measures is evident in the domestic dwelling typology that emerged at this time, the gable-fronted 'Dutch Billy' houses. Representatives of this house type have been identified throughout the city despite extensive modifications and several examples can be found on Capel Street, Middle Abbey Street, Parnell Street and along the quays *(fig. 9)*.

Inspired by Parisian precedents, Ormonde was instrumental in the creation of terraces addressing broad boulevards along the banks of the Liffey, eschewing the traditional placement of buildings backing onto the river's edge. This direct engagement with the river marked the beginning of its perception as a positive urban element. An elegant quayside evolved, establishing a coherent riverine structure which endures today. In 1680 Humphrey Jervis, whose newly acquired lands formed the Jervis estate, developed Ormond Quay and named it in honour of the viceroy. These modest terraces typically comprised three-storey brick houses with concealed basements and enjoyed views over the river. Development of the quayside progressed eastwards, forming Bachelor's Walk, and westwards, to make Inns Quay. Extended river frontage spanning westwards from Church Street to Phoenix Park was leased to William Ellis who subsequently developed Arran Quay. Francis Place's evocative sketch of 1698 captures this work in progress.

Stone from St Mary's Abbey was used in the construction of Essex Bridge in 1678. This link established Capel Street as a central spine within the emerging gridded framework of the Jervis estate and provided a vital connection to

Dame Street and the old city. The bridge was rebuilt in 1872 and is now known as Grattan Bridge. Jervis was also responsible for the construction of Ormond Bridge, crossing the river at Wood Quay. Ormond Market also dates from the late seventeenth century, when the official venue of the City Market was relocated north of the river. The market was demolished in 1892 and Ormond Square, an attractive Dublin Corporation housing scheme, was built in its place in 1921.

Towards the end of the seventeenth century the focus of urban development began to shift eastwards. A number of factors contributed to this trend, among them the fact that the lands surrounding Smithfield retained uses associated with the cattle trade and small industry. This, combined with Ormonde's decision to locate his mansion elsewhere, did nothing to promote the northwest sector as a fashionable place to live. The Moores, earls of Drogheda, acquired a large tract of lands associated with St Mary's Abbey and continued the progression of eastward development initiated by Jervis. This easterly transformation of the cityscape was accelerated by the reclamation of the North Lotts, a sprawling marsh in the area of today's docklands, a project instigated by the City Assembly in 1682 and completed in 1717.

The Eighteenth Century

JERVIS ESTATE
Charles Brooking's map of 1728 indicates the development of the streets around St Mary's Church.

Courtesy of Royal Irish Academy

At the turn of the eighteenth century, development north of the river hinged around the Jervis and Moore estates, with Marlborough Street forming an eastern edge. Capel Street had been set out for residential use in the late seventeenth century, establishing an affluent neighbourhood to rival that of the Aungier estate south of the river. St Mary's Church commanded a prominent position in the new quarter, at the corner of Mary and Jervis streets *(fig. 10)*. The church, which displays one of the earliest galleried interiors in the city, was designed by William Robinson and completed in 1704 by Thomas Burgh.

The Royal Barracks, now Collins Barracks, was initiated by the second Duke of Ormonde on the banks of the Liffey between Oxmantown and Phoenix Park. Designed by the Surveyor General, Thomas Burgh, and completed in 1706, it was reputedly the most impressive barracks of its kind at the time *(fig. 11)*. However the immense scale of the complex, combined with the presence of Smithfield Market and its associated agricultural uses, had the effect of banishing fashionable residential dwellings eastwards. There were some exceptions to this (though few survive), such as Richard Castle's town house for the Earl of Bective (1740), which once dominated the west side of the market.

(fig. 10)
ST MARY'S CHURCH
Wolfe Tone Square
(1704)

Designed by the noted architect, William Robinson, St Mary's was located at the centre of the late seventeenth-century Jervis estate development. It has one of the earliest galleried interiors in Dublin and is now used as a restaurant and bar.

(fig. 11)
COLLINS BARRACKS
Benburb Street
(c.1700, rebuilt c.1770)

Formerly the Royal Barracks, this complex was initiated by the 2nd Duke of Ormonde and funded by a tax on tobacco and beer. An entirely new concept, it was considered the largest and longest-occupied barracks in Europe until vacated by the Irish Army recently. The first recorded building was designed by Thomas Burgh, but the complex was rebuilt by Henry Keene about 1770. The National Museum of Ireland (Decorative Arts and History) is housed here now.

COLLINS BARRACKS
Benburb Street
(c.1700, rebuilt c.1770)

East elevation of west range, Palatine Square.

(fig. 12)
37-39 MONTPELIER HILL
(c.1715)

This is a rare survival of a pair of early eighteenth-century Dutch Billy style houses in Dublin. They were erected about 1715, but the top storey was rebuilt about 2010. The massive shared chimneystack serves corner fireplaces typical of the era and the interior retains an interesting roof structure and original timber panelling.

(fig. 13)
66 CAPEL STREET
(1716-19)

This Dutch Billy is an excellent example of Dublin's rich pre-Georgian domestic architecture, its façade subtly enlivened by diminishing openings, architraves and early replacement windows. The Baroque doorcase is exceptional, and the interior is said to boast some of the most important early wainscoting in the city. The right-hand doorway is a later insertion.

Pockets of more modest housing emerged in the early eighteenth century, among them houses on Montpelier Hill and Capel Street *(fig. 12)*. Many of the original plots along Capel Street were subdivided at this time, allowing terraced two-bay town houses to replace the older city mansions, thus establishing the pattern and scale evident today. 62-67 Capel Street date from this period and 66 is particularly worthy of note. A surviving Dutch Billy house dating from 1723, it boasts an exceptional early eighteenth-century Baroque doorcase, and the interior features some of the most important early wainscoting in the city *(fig. 13)*.

Following land reclamation along the North Lotts, a detailed map of the north quays was

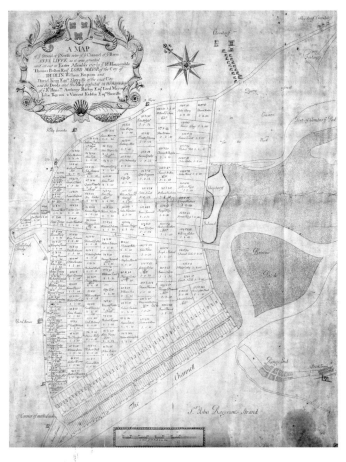

A MAP OF YE NORTH SIDE OF YE CHANNEL OF YE RIVER ANNA LIFFE (1717)

This map of the North Lotts, setting out parcels of ground to be built upon, was issued by the City Assembly.

Courtesy of National Library of Ireland

LUKE GARDINER, M.P., (d.1755), VICE-TREASURER OF IRELAND AND BUILDING DEVELOPER IN DUBLIN

Charles Jervas' portrait of Gardiner, engraved by John Brooks.

© National Gallery of Ireland

issued by the City Assembly in 1717. Proposed land divisions were outlined along an elaborate, orthogonal street network, lined with narrow plots and fronted by a broad quay along the Liffey. Although the plans were only partially implemented and the intended streetscape was severed by the Royal Canal in 1792, the framework for the docklands was firmly ingrained in the city's morphology.

Luke Gardiner (1690-1755), a banker and private developer, later to become a Member of Parliament, Surveyor General of the Customs, Privy Councillor, and Deputy Vice-Treasurer of Ireland, began acquiring land in the early eighteenth century. His first major acquisition was the Moore holding in 1714, comprising a large share of the lands of St Mary's Abbey. In addition, he purchased land from the City Assembly and from the Jervis estate, making him the most substantial landowner north of the river, allowing him to establish the Gardiner estate. Though not part of a greater

(fig. 14)
HENRIETTA STREET
(1729-55)

This street is one of the city's most impressive residential ensembles. It was laid out in 1729-30 by Luke Gardiner and completed in 1755. The architectural historian Christine Casey describes the houses as 'grand, bare and somewhat grim, their great brick barn-like elevations, largely unadorned but for the sober stone doorcases'.

(fig. 15)
4 HENRIETTA STREET
(1740s, remodelled
1780s)

This house was altered internally in the late eighteenth century following the marriage of Lady Harriet Farnham to Denis Daly of Dunsandle, Co. Galway.

urban plan his development of Henrietta Street in the 1720s was an innovative and influential model for eighteenth-century housing development in Dublin. Following the tradition of seventeenth-century practice in London and the setting out of St Stephen's Green in 1664, generous plots were laid out, but long-term leases were not issued until a house was constructed *(figs. 14-15)*. Peppercorn, or nominal, rents were charged for the first eighteen months to encourage prompt development of the plots and, over subsequent decades, fifteen houses were built, thirteen of which remain. Eminent architects, among them Edward Lovett Pearce and Richard Castle, were involved in their design. With some exceptions, the houses were plain in their external expression, presenting unadorned red brick façades that concealed opulent interiors with grand staircases and ornate decorative plasterwork.

(fig. 16)
9 HENRIETTA STREET
(1731)

Regarded as the finest
house on the street
and one of the best
houses in Dublin, No.
9 was likely designed
by Edward Lovett
Pearce for Thomas
Carter, Master of the
Rolls from 1725-54. It
was modelled very
closely on 30 Old
Burlington Street,
London, town house
of Algernon Coote,
Lord Mountrath. It
has a grand entrance
hall and superb
plasterwork.

The sumptuous
staircase hall.

9 Henrietta Street (1731) is one of the most
impressive eighteenth-century town houses in
the city *(fig. 16)*. Generally considered to be
the work of Edward Lovett Pearce, its design
was influenced by 30 Old Burlington Street,
London, built by Lord Burlington and Colen
Campbell (1713). The interior displays
stunning plasterwork and a palatial entrance
hall featuring a cantilevered Portland stone
staircase. The plasterwork in number 10

The hall, from the
first floor landing.

*Courtesy of Irish
Architectural Archive*

(fig. 17)
10 HENRIETTA STREET
(Late 1720s)

Luke Gardiner built this house for his own family. The four rightmost bays are the original house and the rest was built for his son, Charles, in 1755. There is fine joinery and plasterwork to the interior.

Internal doorway.

Courtesy of Irish Architectural Archive

Room at the rear of the ground floor.

Courtesy of Irish Architectural Archive

(Blessington House) is also noteworthy *(fig. 17)*. It was built by the first Luke Gardiner as his family home in 1730. Pearce also had a hand in the design of this house, which was extended in 1755 and extensively remodelled in the nineteenth century.

The scale and elegance of the Henrietta Street houses attracted wealthy tenants, introducing an unprecedented level of grandeur and setting a new standard for domestic ventures in the city. This scale of building was paralleled on Dominick Street, with leases issued by Lady Dominick in the 1750s. Number 20 is of particular importance, due to the extraordinary high-relief Rococo plasterwork displayed within *(fig. 18)*.

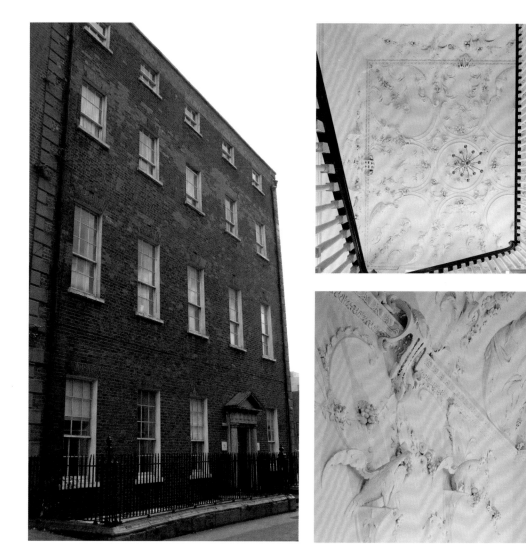

(fig. 18)
YOUTH WORK IRELAND
20 Dominick Street
(1758-60)

Christine Casey describes this as 'the most astonishing example of the characteristic Dublin townhouse – a sober and somewhat ungainly brick envelope devoid of ornament enclosing a sumptuously decorated interior'.

Ceiling to the stairs hall.

(fig. 19)
TYRONE HOUSE
(Department of
Education)
Marlborough Street
(1740)

This mansion was
designed for Marcus
Beresford by Richard
Castle. A matching
building was added to
the north in 1835
when Tyrone House
and its grounds were
acquired by the Board
of Education.

TYRONE HOUSE

Tyrone House, on Marlborough Street, is another prominent city mansion dating from this period, designed by Richard Castle and completed in 1740 for Marcus Beresford, Viscount Tyrone *(fig. 19)*. The superb interior stucco work is commonly attributed to the Lafranchini brothers.

Gardiner's aspirations to create an élite residential enclave were further realised in his development of Sackville Street (now O'Connell Street), named after his own son *(fig. 20)*. Described by the artist James Malton as 'the noblest street in Dublin', it was lined with elegant mansions overlooking Gardiner's

SACKVILLE MALL
(c.1760)

A drawing by Oliver Grace, showing the original appearance of O'Connell Street before the development of Parnell Square.

Courtesy of National Library of Ireland

(fig. 20)
42 O'CONNELL STREET
(1752)
The only surviving eighteenth-century house on this grand thoroughfare, built for Robert Robinson, State Physician and Professor of Anatomy at Trinity College. It was designed by Richard Castle and the interior plasterwork is by Robert West.

Mall, an enclosed landscaped space along the centre, punctuated with obelisks. The composition of this street and its celebrated promenade formed an urban set-piece that was much lauded overseas and set the scale for central Dublin.

(fig. 21)
ROTUNDA HOSPITAL
Parnell Square
(1751-7)

The Lying-in Hospital was commissioned by Dr Bartholomew Mosse and designed by Richard Castle and John Ensor. It was the first purpose-built charitable maternity hospital in Ireland or Britain.

To the north of Sackville Street, Dr Batholomew Mosse was planning his Lying-in Hospital and in 1748 he commissioned Richard Castle to design the building *(fig. 21)*. To fund this charitable venture he created the New Gardens adjacent to the proposed site of the hospital. This was a pleasure garden designed for elaborate parties and concerts, to which the public paid an entrance fee. By 1757, the hospital was complete, but built off-axis with Sackville Street, a move that drew some criticism, but which allowed a connection to the primary northern route into the city, Dorset Street.

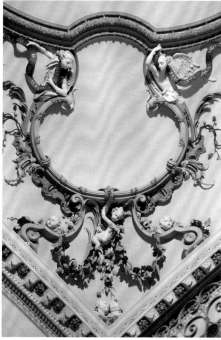

**ROTUNDA HOSPITAL
CHAPEL**
(1751-7)

The hospital chapel is
an exuberant Baroque
masterpiece, featuring
the extraordinary
work of Flemish
stuccodore
Bartholomew
Cramillion.

**THE NEW GARDENS
AND SACKVILLE
MALL**
Parnell Square
(1748)

This pleasure garden,
to which the public
paid an admittance
fee, was established
by Dr Bartholomew
Mosse to fund the
construction of his
Lying-in Hospital. It is
depicted here on John
Rocque's map of
1756. The gardens
survived until
encroached upon in
the 1940s by the
expansion of the
hospital.

*Reproduced with the
permission of the
Board of Trinity College
Dublin*

Cavendish Street (now Cavendish Row) was
followed by Palace Row to the north and by
Granby Row to the west, completing Rutland
Square, known today as Parnell Square. The
prominent placement of John Ensor's Rotunda

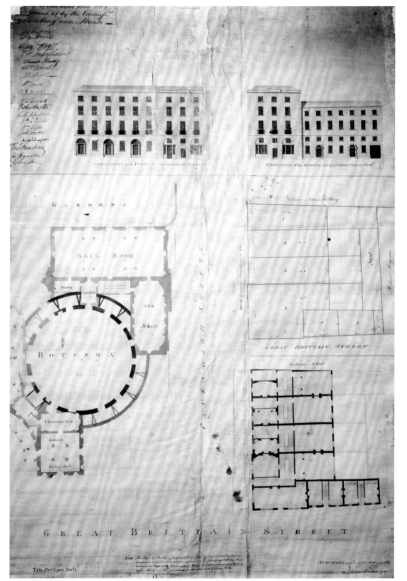

CAVENDISH ROW
(1787)

Wide Streets Commissioners' proposal for Cavendish Row, showing plans of buildings on this side of Parnell Square and on Great Britain Street (Parnell Street). The layout of the Rotunda complex is shown at left in the drawing.

Courtesy of Dublin City Library and Archive

(1764) and Richard Johnston's New Assembly Rooms (1784) at the corner of Cavendish Row, went some way towards resolving the problematic vista from Sackville Street *(figs. 22-3)*. Designed with lavish interiors, as an extension to the gardens and a venue for functions, the buildings today house the Gate and Ambassador theatres.

(fig. 22)
AMBASSADOR THEATRE *(formerly Rotunda)* and **GATE THEATRE** *(formerly New Assembly Rooms)*
Parnell Square
(1764-86)

The Round Room (or Rotunda) was designed by John Ensor in a spartan brick and rendered style that was refaced in stucco and Coade stone in 1786 with a classical frieze of bucrania and garlands. The New Assembly Rooms were designed by Richard Johnston and built robustly in granite, with a Doric portico of Portland stone.

Detail of the bucrania (ox skulls) and swags to the cornice.

(fig. 23)
GATE THEATRE
Parnell Square
(1786)

The former New
Assembly Rooms
became the Gate
Theatre in 1928 and
was designed in the
style of a palazzo with
a porticoed front.

Lord Charlemont chose the elevated central plots on Palace Row, overlooking the New Gardens, to build his town house. Designed by William Chambers in 1763, Charlemont House addresses a modest forecourt with balustraded quadrant wings, and exhibits exquisite stonework, testament to the skilled craft of master mason, Simon Vierpyl *(fig. 24)*. The building was remodelled in 1933 by Horace O'Rourke, to accommodate the Hugh Lane Municipal Art Gallery. With the establishment of Rutland Square and Charlemont House, a proliferation of new streets subsequently appeared in the north-eastern quarter of the city, among them Summerhill, Gardiner's Row, Temple Street and Eccles Street.

The Pillar Room,
formerly the
ballroom of the
Rotunda complex,
has Adamesque
detailing.

(fig. 24)
**DUBLIN CITY
GALLERY
(THE HUGH LANE)**

Parnell Square North
(Begun 1763)

This grand town
house for Lord
Charlemont was
designed by William
Chambers, with
Simon Vierpyl as
master-mason, John
Ivory as principal
carpenter and
Christopher Plummer
as bricklayer. The
rounded forecourt
provides a fine
setting. It was
remodelled as an art
gallery in the 1930s.

The hall has splendid
Corinthian columns.

Stairs hall.

Despite grandiose ambitions, the process of buying and developing land in segments meant that Gardiner's building ventures were disparate and disconnected. It remained the role of his grandson, the second Luke Gardiner, Lord Mountjoy, as a private developer and a member of the Wide Streets Commission, to creatively rationalise the fragmentary plan of the north city. John Rocque's map of Dublin (1756) is a portrait of the city before the dramatic urban transformation driven by the Commissioners and key developers like Gardiner and Fitzwilliam. The Commission had been established in 1757 by an Act of Parliament, specifically to deal with the formation of Parliament Street and of a route from Essex Bridge to Dublin Castle, but its members played a pivotal role in coordinating the development of the city up to the early nineteenth century. The Commissioners were also charged with tackling the problem of congestion and were granted considerable powers to respond to the emerging drive for orthogonal layouts and regularity in urban form. With the exception of the Lord Mayor, all the Commissioners were Members of Parliament. While some of them undoubtedly used their positions to further their own private interests, they were also driven by noble motives and their drawings and minute books demonstrate an awareness of architectural theory and a desire to emulate Continental trends.

Leases for North Great George's Street were issued in 1769, defining a pocket of development within the expansive Gardiner estate belonging to the Archdall family *(figs. 25-6)*. Robert West's Belvedere House (1786) completed the composition of this fine

(fig. 25)
21 DENMARK STREET GREAT AND 51 NORTH GREAT GEORGE'S STREET (c.1790 and 1768)

The turning of the corner of these Georgian streets is cleverly designed. The North Great George's Street house and the end of its neighbour on Denmark Street present a symmetrical five-bay frontage.

(fig. 26)
MAHAFFY HOUSE 38 North Great George's Street (c.1785)

(fig. 27)
BELVEDERE HOUSE
Denmark Street Great
(c.1770-86)

Robert West designed this grand house for the first Earl of Belvedere. The second earl, George Rochfort offered the incomplete house for sale in 1777, but later decided to reside there.

Michael Stapleton, the renowned stuccadore, who was Robert West's executor, was responsible for the decoration of the stairs hall, one of the finest interiors in the city.

Courtesy of Irish Architectural Archive

street by providing an elegant landmark at its northern end *(fig. 27)*. The interiors of the house are enriched by exceptional neoclassical plasterwork attributed to master stuccodore Michael Stapleton.

BELVEDERE HOUSE

*Courtesy of Irish
Architectural Archive*

Urban growth accelerated in the last quarter of the century and was reflected in a remarkable population rise, from 129,000 in 1771 to 200,000 in 1800. This was a period of unprecedented and enlightened progress, embracing urban design as well as architecture. For the first time the city was being regarded as a cohesive whole. The Wide Streets Commissioners sought inspiration overseas, with the city surveyor, Thomas Sherrard, who was employed as secretary, clerk and surveyor to the Commission from 1782, being dispatched on occasion to review contemporary design precedents in Britain and Continental Europe. Like many of the Commissioners, Gardiner displayed an interest in matters artistic and architectural, commissioning artworks from an early age. He embarked on a *Grand Tour* in 1770-72, travelling extensively through France and Italy and it is arguable that these travels may have inspired some of his *grands projets*, such as Mountjoy Square and the proposed (but unexecuted) Royal Circus. Such schemes signalled a progression from the Baroque emphasis on grandiose focal points to a more organic neoclassical approach, allowing the manipulation of existing geometries and the creation of formulated views and vistas.

JAMES JOYCE
CULTURAL CENTRE

(fig. 28)
**JAMES JOYCE
CULTURAL CENTRE**
35 North Great
George's Street
(1784)

A typical three-bay
house on this fine
Georgian street.

The plain brick façades that lined the streets and squares of the city echoed the wider Palladian revival in Ireland, introduced in the 1720s by architects such as Pearce and Castle. The refined terraces displayed a stage-set quality that provided a neutral backdrop for the changes in the urban landscape that were emerging in the eighteenth-century fabric. However, the practice of speculative development within the private estates led to the construction of houses in groups of two, three or four, which ruled out strict uniformity and resulted in a rich and subtle variety of scale, typology and palette of materials. The typical eighteenth-century Dublin town house, with its classical doorcase, was otherwise without external ornamentation, unlike its London counterpart that commonly featured decorative embellishments. However, these sober exteriors often conceal sumptuous interiors, with exemplary plasterwork by skilled craftsmen, among them Bartholomew Cramillion, Robert West, Michael Stapleton and Charles Thorp *(fig. 28)*.

(fig. 29)
1 MOUNTJOY SQUARE NORTH (1792)

The corner property was formerly three houses, built by Arthur Burdett, who leased the plot in 1791. The ground floor was re-faced in 1902 for the ancient Order of Hibernians. The terraces surrounding Mountjoy Square were ingeniously folded in to anchor the corners and terminate the approaching vista, providing a sense of enclosure to the central space.

The 1790s saw a remarkable flourishing of construction in the north-eastern sector of the city where Gardiner skilfully expanded his vast estate and strategically acquired lands to realise his urban vision on a grand scale. A number of critical developments came to fruition in this period, among them the continuation of Sackville Street to the river and the construction of Carlisle Bridge in 1795 (replaced in 1880 and renamed O'Connell Bridge). The extension of Sackville Street effectively changed the nature of the street from residential to commercial. There was also the development of North Frederick Street on the 'Barley Fields', linking Sackville Street to the Great Northern Road (Dorset Street), and the development of Gardiner Street, Gloucester (now Seán McDermott) Street, Mountjoy Square and associated streets *(fig. 29)*.

MOUNTJOY SQUARE WEST

Thomas Sherrard drew up this unexecuted design for Luke Gardiner, for a 'palace front' for the west side of Mountjoy Square, in 1787.

Courtesy of Dublin City Library and Archive

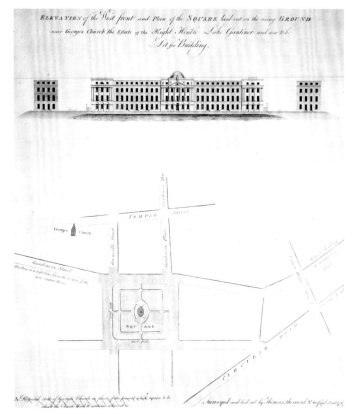

Gardiner had ambitious plans for Mountjoy Square, the proposed west elevation of which appears on a drawing by Thomas Sherrard in 1787. His aspiration comprised a singular monumental stone-clad façade featuring a central pedimented bay and dome, flanked by symmetrical end pavilions. This composition was undoubtedly influenced by various residential ventures in Britain, among them Bedford Square in London (1783). The construction of Robert Adam's Charlotte Square, Edinburgh (1791-1807) was contemporaneous with that of Mountjoy Square and provides an interesting parallel. The practice of speculative development of plots meant that Gardiner's monumental proposals were abandoned, but Mountjoy Square, a perfect square measuring 600 feet along each side, remains a pivotal plan-unit in the evolution of the eighteenth-century city. Sited on a plateau, with views of the city and mountains to the south, the square tied together a number of disparate urban set-pieces, connecting the proposed Royal Circus to the north with the Custom House to the south and Rutland Square to the west.

ROYAL CIRCUS

Leases were issued in 1792 for this proposed urban set-piece at the west end of Eccles Street. However, the Mater Hospital was built on the site in 1861, although Eccles Street and the notable kink of Blessington Street/Berkeley Road reflect the surviving prongs of the trident-like arrangement that had been envisaged.

From William Wilson's Modern Plan of the City and Environs of Dublin (1798).

Reproduced with the permission of the Board of Trinity College Dublin

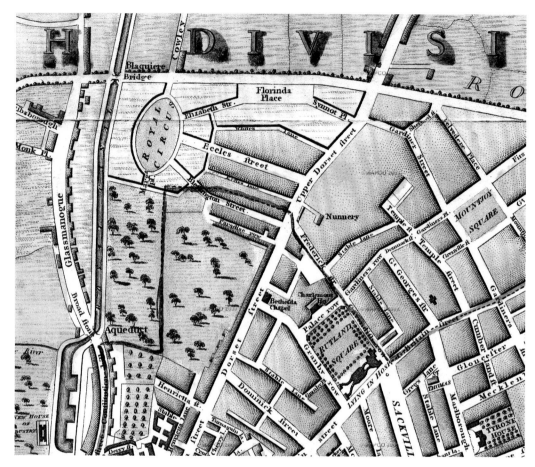

Plans for Gardiner's Royal Circus were being finalised when construction began on Mountjoy Square in the early 1790s, and leases for the Circus were issued in 1792. The proposal comprised an ellipse of grand mansions composed around a central landscaped garden, surpassing those of Mountjoy Square in magnificence and scale. Francis Johnston, who lived in Eccles Street and who was the architect of St George's Church, Hardwicke Place (1806), may have been involved. As in the Piazza del Popolo in Rome and Place d'Armes in Versailles, three streets were to radiate from the oval, in the form of a trident. This scheme was intended to give coherence to an estate that had expanded in an irregular fashion. Though the circus never materialised, it dominated street directory maps for decades, and traces of its routes remain legible in today's streetscape.

(fig. 30) (top)
DUBLIN TAKEN NEAR THE CUSTOM HOUSE, 1817

An evocative view, by Thomas Sautelle Roberts, engraved by Robert Havell the Elder and Robert Havell the Younger, showing Gandon's Custom House in its original busy riverine setting.

© *National Gallery of Ireland*

OLD CUSTOM HOUSE
Wellington Quay
(1704)

Brooking's map of 1728 illustrated the precursor of the Custom House, which stood on what is now Wellington Quay on the south side of the Liffey, close to Grattan Bridge.

Courtesy of Royal Irish Academy

CUSTOM HOUSE

Custom House Quay/Beresford Place (1791)
The grand quayside entrance to this most iconic of Dublin riverside buildings.

The Beresford Place front.

Cast of riverine head representing the Atlantic.

Courtesy of Irish Architectural Archive

The siting of the new Custom House (1791) at Beresford Place consolidated the eastern expansion. The controversial decision to locate the building along the north-eastern quays had the effect of shifting the urban focus from the medieval core, where the original Custom House had stood. The move was of particular strategic interest to Gardiner and his brother-in-law, Beresford, both Wide Streets Commissioners with a vested interest in the area. The placement of the Custom House permitted the construction of Carlisle Bridge, which facilitated movement between the developed estates north and south of the river but prevented the passage of ships into the historic core. The Custom House was James Gandon's first large-scale commission in Ireland and is a magnificent neoclassical essay in civic building. Described by Maurice Craig as 'a beautiful study in overlapping symmetries', the river-front façade was clad in Portland stone and features a central pedimented portico and domed cupola *(fig. 30)*. Rich sculptural embellishments include Edward Smyth's riverine head keystones.

Detail of internal doorway.

CUSTOM HOUSE

Main stairway.

CUSTOM HOUSE AND BERESFORD PLACE

An aerial photograph from about 1939, showing the busy quayside at the Custom House, Beresford Place to the north and a row of three later buildings that helped continue the eighteenth-century crescent on the site of current Busáras. The vacant site to the east now accommodates part of the IFSC office quarter.

Courtesy of Irish Architectural Archive

(fig. 31)
1-5 BERESFORD PLACE
(c.1793)

This curving terrace of five houses was designed by James Gandon in 1792 and built the following year. It provides a fitting, if incomplete, backdrop for his Custom House. The southern house had its façades altered about 1930.

PORTRAIT OF JAMES GANDON (1743-1823), ARCHITECT, c.1786-c.1796

Gandon, as painted by William Cuming and Tilly Kettle.

© *National Gallery of Ireland*

Opposite the north, garden front of the building is Beresford Place, a row of five houses built by Gandon in 1793 for John Beresford. A larger crescent of houses had been planned but was not executed *(fig. 31)*. Gandon was also responsible for the design of the Four Courts (1776-1802), a project initiated by Thomas Cooley *(fig. 32)*.

(fig. 32)
FOUR COURTS
Inns Quay
(1776-1802)

Thomas Cooley
initiated works to
house the Public
Record Office and
Gandon took over in
1784 when it was
decided to move the
law courts to the site.

Conceived as a Public Records Office, the decision was made in 1784 to accommodate the law courts, at which point Gandon took over the project. Both the Custom House and the Four Courts were reduced to smouldering shells during the War of Independence and the Civil War and were rebuilt in the 1920s.

FOUR COURTS

The screen to one of
the front courtyards.

Interior of the domed
hall.

(fig. 33)
**THE LAW SOCIETY
OF IRELAND**
Blackhall Place
(1773-85)

Thomas Ivory's
Bluecoat School
succeeded the
Hospital and Free
School of Charles II of
1671. Ivory's design
had included a
steeple and a
quadrangle, the
former appearing as a
squat cupola in 1894
and the latter not
executed.

Another significant public building dating from this period is Thomas Ivory's Bluecoat School (1773-85) on Blackhall Place, now housing the Law Society of Ireland *(fig. 33)*. The formal Palladian façade offers a framed vista from Blackhall Street, the effect of which has been diluted following the loss of Georgian fabric in the mid-twentieth century. The chapel, now the President's Hall, was designed by Ivory and built in 1773 *(fig. 34)*.

*Courtesy of Irish
Architectural Archive*

(fig. 34)
THE PRESIDENT'S HALL
Blackhall Place
(1773-85)

The robust exterior to the chapel of the Bluecoat School

The former chapel of the Bluecoat School has paired Corinthian pilasters that flanked the altar. The stained-glass window (1936), by Evie Hone, represents the Risen Christ.

(fig. 35)
THIRD LOCK, ROYAL CANAL
Off Whitworth Road
(c.1795)

The Royal Canal, begun in 1790, is one of the two great manmade waterways in Ireland, stretching from Dublin Bay to the Shannon. It was costly to build and was never a commercial success. It was bought at a bargain price by the Midland and Great Western Railway Company, which had proposed to fill it in and build their railway line over it, but they eventually settled for having a track alongside the canal.

(fig. 36)
ASHTOWN BRIDGE
(formerly Longford Bridge)
(1792)

This bridge is typical of many on the Royal Canal. It is robustly built of limestone, with little decorative detail. The cartouche reads 'Longford Bridge 1792'.

The municipal boundary to the north was defined by the Royal Canal, constructed to connect the Liffey in Dublin to the Shannon at Richmond Harbour, Cloondara, Co. Longford. Work on the canal began in 1790 and the Dublin section was substantially complete by 1817 *(figs. 35-6)*.

The Phoenix Park contained any western expansion along the Liffey. Though a major re-working of the park structure did not happen until the following century, the eighteenth century saw a number of significant developments. Among the military works carried out was the construction of the Magazine Fort by John Corneille in 1738, with later alterations by Francis Johnston *(fig. 37)*. At the centre of the park stands the Phoenix Monument, the bird crowning a Corinthian column that stands on a pedestal bearing the coat of arms of Lord Chesterfield *(fig. 38)*.

DUBLIN FROM THE PHOENIX PARK, LOOKING EAST, 1753

Joseph Tudor's evocative view of the south side of Phoenix Park, with the village of Islandbridge in the middle distance. The Magazine Fort, designed by John Corneille in 1738, stands on the hill to the left. Emphasizing its origins as a deer-park, a stag appears between the trees at the left hand side.

Courtesy of Andrew Bonar Law

(fig. 37)
MAGAZINE FORT
Phoenix Park
(1738 and later)

This distinctive military installation, in the form of a 'star fort', stands on high ground at the south side of Phoenix Park.

Courtesy of the Photographic Unit, DAHG

(fig. 38)
PHOENIX MONUMENT
Chesterfield Avenue
Phoenix Park
(1747)

The Earl of Chesterfield had this Portland stone monument built in 1747. It has been moved several times, but now stands at its original location.

Coat of arms of Lord Chesterfield.

Eighteenth-century residences in the park include Mountjoy House (1728), built as a suburban villa for the Gardiner family. It became a barracks in 1780 and has been the headquarters of the Ordnance Survey since 1825 *(fig. 39)*. Áras an Uachtaráin, the official residence of the President of Ireland, began life as the Vice-Regal Lodge in 1782 *(fig. 40)*.

(fig. 39)
MOUNTJOY HOUSE
Ordnance Survey Office
Phoenix Park
(1728)

This house was originally built for Luke Gardiner as a suburban villa. It was converted to a military barracks in 1780 and has been the headquarters of the Ordnance Survey since 1825.

Courtesy of Irish Architectural Archive

(fig. 40)
ÁRAS AN UACHTARÁIN
Phoenix Park
(1782)

The official residence of the President of Ireland was built in 1752-7 as a dwelling for Nathaniel Clements, Park Ranger and was enlarged in 1782 for use by the British viceroy in Ireland. The Palladian mansion was later flanked by nineteenth-century single-storey wings that were later heightened. The entrance hall is similar to that at Westport House, Co. Mayo and the Lords' Chamber in the old Parliament House in College Green, Dublin.

Courtesy of Photographic Unit, DAHG

The Nineteenth Century

(fig. 41)
**O'CONNELL
MONUMENT**
O'Connell Street
Lower
(1883)

The monument to
Daniel O'Connell is
one of the best-
known landmarks in
central Dublin,
standing at O'Connell
Bridge and signalling
the entry to the
principal grand
thoroughfare.

SYNNOTT PLACE
(c.1800)

This terrace marks the
northern edge of the
Georgian city, its line
a relic of the
unexecuted Royal
Circus.

The nineteenth century was a time of considerable political, religious and social change in Dublin. Significant advances in road and rail communications established it as a thriving commercial city in the latter half of the century, but this economic success coincided with social decline and a deepening housing crisis. The changing political face of the country is reflected in the iconography of the city, most notably in O'Connell Street where the statue of Daniel O'Connell, 'The Liberator' (John Henry Foley, 1883) and the early twentieth-century monument to Parnell bookend the south and north ends of this historic streetscape *(fig. 41)*.

The portrait of Dublin at the opening of the nineteenth century is that of a resplendent capital city, with a coherent framework of streets and squares and architecture to rival that of cities in Britain and elsewhere in Europe. The Act of Union, passed in 1801, prompted the gradual departure of many Members of Parliament and of the aristocratic classes, and with them the demand for grand city residences and the associated luxury trades. Despite the profound effect that this political and societal shift had on the workings of the city, building continued in the early decades of the new century, but on a more modest scale. The eastward expansion that had been initiated towards the end of the eighteenth century continued and several key streets were developed, including Gardiner Street, which had its origins in the 1790s and connected Mountjoy Square to the Custom House. Though leases for Mountjoy Square were issued as early as 1792, a failure to fulfil contractual obligations, on the part of several developers, resulted in prolonged delays, and the square was not complete until 1818.

(fig. 42)
ST GEORGE'S CHURCH
Hardwicke Place
(1802-13)

St George's is considered to be Francis Johnston's best architectural set-piece. Its Ionic portico graces a building that is broader than it is long, closing the vista in a delta-like arrangement of streets.

The eighteenth-century focus on establishing a coherent and elegant street structure continued, with a number of urban set-pieces emerging and constructed vistas arranged around a focal point, typically a church. St George's in Hardwicke Place, designed by Francis Johnston, was one such composition *(fig. 42)*. Completed in 1813, the church was centrally placed within an elegant crescent of houses, terminating the vista along Hardwicke Street from North Frederick Street. This elegant neoclassical granite building is a

(fig. 43)
PAVEE POINT *(formerly The Free Church)*
Charles Street Great
(1800)

This robustly designed Methodist chapel, built to accommodate a congregation of 1,000, was converted in 1990 to house the Dublin Travellers' Education and Development Group.

Dublin landmark, its spire visible across the north city. In a similar manner, the Wesleyan Methodist Church on Charles Street, known as the Free Church, closed the view from Summer Hill along Rutland Street Upper (Seán O'Casey Avenue) *(fig. 43)*. These vistas have since been obscured, but the street patterns and design intentions are still evident. An enduring example is Semple's Black Church on St Mary's Place, built in 1830. A solemn essay in calp limestone and flanked by pinnacled buttresses, the church forms an impressive centrepiece around which the surrounding streets pivot *(fig. 44)*.

With the exception of large infrastructural projects, nineteenth-century developments did not radically alter the character or structure of the established city. The Royal and Grand canals encircled the city, creating a strong physical edge between the core and the suburbs. Interventions worked within existing fabric, buildings were remodelled and plots intensified. Some plots were amalgamated to accommodate hotels, schools, offices and institutions. Within this formula however, there was still scope for singular architectural expression.

(fig. 44)
'THE BLACK CHURCH'
Mountjoy Street/St Mary's Place North (1830)

St Mary's Church of Ireland church, by John Semple and Son, is the subject of a tradition that a person, walking three times anti-clockwise around the building at midnight while reciting the 'Hail Mary', will see the devil.

An empty plot, adjacent to Nelson's Pillar (Thomas Kirk, 1809, destroyed 1966), was selected in 1814 for the new General Post Office. Built four years later to designs by Francis Johnston, it occupied the full width of an urban block on Sackville Street *(fig. 45)*. The building was the rebel headquarters during the 1916 Easter Rising and suffered substantial damage. It was extensively rebuilt in 1929, but Johnston's Ionic portico remains a monumental centrepiece on Dublin's principal thoroughfare.

(fig. 45)
GPO (GENERAL POST OFFICE)
O'Connell Street Lower
(1818)

This monumental public building, one of the city's great set-pieces, has iconic status because it was the headquarters of the rebels during the Easter Rising of 1916. Designed by Francis Johnston, it was remodelled in three phases between 1904 and 1915 by J. Howard Pentland. A burnt-out shell after the Rising, it was rebuilt in 1924-9 by a team headed by T.J. Byrne.

Courtesy of Andrew Bonar Law

GPO (GENERAL POST OFFICE)
O'Connell Street
Lower

GPO

The statues over the portico represent Mercury, Hibernia and Fidelity.

Open parkland at Constitution Hill became the site of the new King's Inns, the centre of legal practice in Ireland. The complex was begun in 1800 by James Gandon and completed in 1817 by Francis Johnston. The main façade was extended to the each side by Frederick Darley in 1846 and Jacob Owen in 1849. At the Henrietta Street side Johnston added a triumphal arch entrance in 1820 *(figs. 46-7)*. This was followed by the addition of the adjacent Law Library by Frederick Darley in 1828, on the site of Archbishop Boulter's house of 1730 *(fig. 48)*. The Italianate appearance and granite façade relate to Gandon's King's Inns rather than the red brick terraced houses of Henrietta Street, but both it and the triumphal arch contribute richly to the composition of the eighteenth-century street.

(fig. 46)
KING'S INNS
Constitution Hill
(1800-49)

The King's Inns complex was constructed to designs by various architects, from James Gandon in 1800 to Jacob Owen in 1849. The doorways are flanked by caryatids.

Gandon's dining hall, the only intact interior designed by him, is a distinguished neoclassical space.

(fig. 47)
KING'S INNS
Henrietta Street
(1817)

Francis Johnston's triumphal arch gateway finishes the city side of the complex.

(fig. 48)
LAW LIBRARY
Henrietta Street
(1825-8)

The site of Archbishop Boulter's early eighteenth-century mansion was acquired by the benchers of King's Inns in 1823. Frederick Darley's library was extended northwards by one bay by James Fuller about 1890. The building bears a resemblance to Iveagh House on St Stephen's Green.

Church building intensified in the first half of the nineteenth century, following a series of Catholic Relief Acts passed in the preceding century which permitted the construction of Catholic churches. After Catholic Emancipation in 1829 there was a further surge in church building. Unlike the buildings of the Church of Ireland, which typically acted as urban markers, Catholic churches were usually placed on less prominent sites, this pattern prevailing even after 1829. With some exceptions, they assumed a neoclassical architecture, perhaps setting themselves apart from the Gothic associated with the 'Established Church'. St Mary's Pro-Cathedral (formerly the Metropolitan Chapel) on Marlborough Street became an exemplar for nineteenth-century Catholic churches *(fig. 49)*. This imposing structure, attributed to John Sweetman, was completed in 1825. The Greek Doric portico, executed in Portland stone and mounted on a raised granite plinth, dominates the modest scale of the streetscape it addresses. The Greek Revival interior is crowned by a central coffered dome and features a classical colonnade and stuccoed apse.

(fig. 49)
ST MARY'S PRO-CATHEDRAL
Marlborough Street
(1814-25, extended several times)

Originally named the Metropolitan Chapel, the Pro-Cathedral was erected by Archbishop Troy before Catholic Emancipation (1829) to replace an earlier building on Liffey Street. Its design owes much to French architecture, especially the church of St Philippe du Roule in Paris. It was altered or added to until as late as 1928.

(fig. 50)
CHURCH OF ST FRANCIS XAVIER
Gardiner Street Upper
(1829-32)

One of John B. Keane's finest churches, its façade modelled on the front of the church of Notre Dame de Lorette in Paris and its interior reflecting that of the Jesuits' mother church, the Gesù, in Rome.

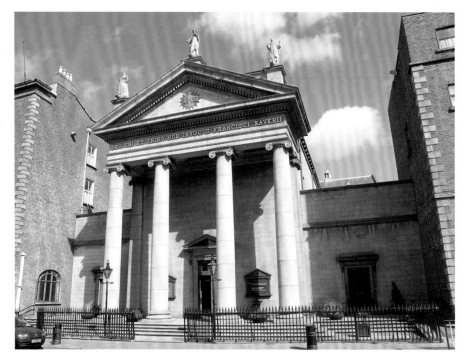

The splendid reredos and altar table. The latter was claimed by the church's builder, Fr Bartholomew Esmonde, to have porphyry panels from the ruins of Nero's Golden House and the altar of the church of San Paolo fuori le Mura in Rome.

The Jesuit church of St Francis Xavier, by John B. Keane, is a post-Emancipation church built in the classical idiom and representative of a newly found confidence within the Catholic Church *(fig. 50)*. Built in 1832 on a large undeveloped stretch of land on Gardiner Street Upper, the site became a significant ecclesiastical centre with the addition of a presbytery, a convent and associated teaching and parochial facilities. Considered one of the finest churches of the period, the Greek Ionic portico in granite ashlar displays Portland stone statues and rests on a shallow stepped podium. The plan borrows from the Gesù, the Jesuit mother church in Rome, having a nave with low side chapels, shallow transepts and a deep apsidal chancel. This elegant church

(fig. 51)
ST PAUL'S CHURCH
Arran Quay
(1835-44)

Patrick Byrne appears
to have modelled his
landmark church on
the north quays on St
Mary's, Moorfields,
London.

retains a refined presence amongst the later
built-up terraces. The influence of St Francis
Xavier's is evident in the design of St Paul's
Church, by Patrick Byrne, prominently sited on
Arran Quay. Completed in 1844, it presents a
pedimented portico in granite ashlar and an
Italianate bell tower surmounted by a copper
dome, forming a distinctive landmark on the
western approach to the city centre *(fig. 51)*.

(fig. 52)
**ST SAVIOUR'S
CHURCH**
Dominick Street
Lower
(1853-61)

This is regarded as
the finest Dublin
example of the work
of the eminent church
architect, J.J.
McCarthy. It is
adjoined to the north
by the Dominican
priory of 1884-7.

The pointed arcade
of clustered columns
has sculpted
Dominican saints to
the spandrels.

The Gothic style dominated church design in the second half of the century. St Saviour's Church on Dominick Street (1856) was designed by J.J. McCarthy and is an excellent example of the Gothic Revival, complete with finely wrought stone masonry and a delightful interior lined with Bath stone *(fig. 52)*. The calp limestone priory to the north was added in 1887 by J.L. Robinson. Another example in this idiom is the Abbey Presbyterian Church, known as Findlater's Church, occupying a pivotal corner on the elevated north side of Parnell Square, terminating the vistas from O'Connell Street and Mountjoy Square *(fig. 53)*. Designed by Scottish architect, Andrew Heiton, it was influenced by French Gothic architecture and displays a wealth of accomplished Gothic detailing.

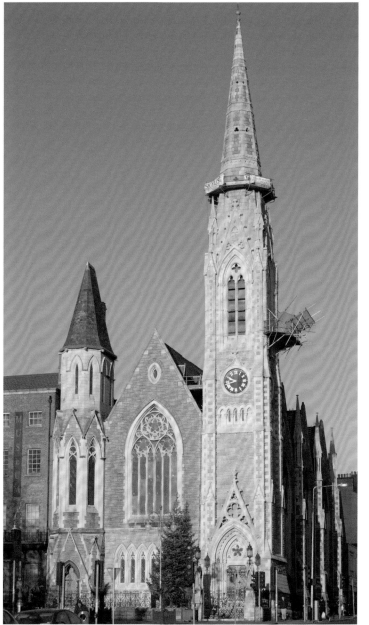

(fig. 53)
**FINDLATER'S
CHURCH**
Parnell Square
(1862-4)

This church was
financed by Dublin
merchant, Alexander
Findlater. Officially
named Abbey
Presbyterian Church,
this distinctive
landmark terminates
the vista at the north
end of O'Connell
Street. The porch and
entrance gate display
masonry, sculpture
and wrought ironwork
of a very high order.

(fig. 54)
MONASTERY OF OUR LADY OF CHARITY OF REFUGE
63-72 Seán McDermott Street
(c.1811, enlarged 1877, 1888)

Now in use as a youth centre, the former Gloucester Street Laundry was the last of Ireland's Magdalene laundries operating when it closed in 1996. The institutional nature of the building is softened by the architectural details that break it up visually and add colour and contrast.

The chapel of 1885, attributed to W.H. Byrne, has a very fine neoclassical interior.

In addition to the abundance of churches, a large number of institutions were founded across the city, reinforcing a drive for social improvement and the provision of public infrastructure. These efforts materialised in the form of schools, convents, hospitals and prisons, in addition to the improvements to services and transport networks *(figs. 54-5)*.

(fig. 55)
**ST PETER'S
PRESBYTERY**
Cabra Road
(c.1835-47, extended
c.1857-65)

This castellated
structure was built as
St Peter's National
Schools. The left-most
block was added
about 1857-65 to link
it with the adjacent St
Peter's Church. It may
have been designed
by Jacob Owen as it
resembles his stable
block at Dublin Castle.

The garden elevation
looks dramatically
different, with its
rendered façade,
although the general
detailing is matched.

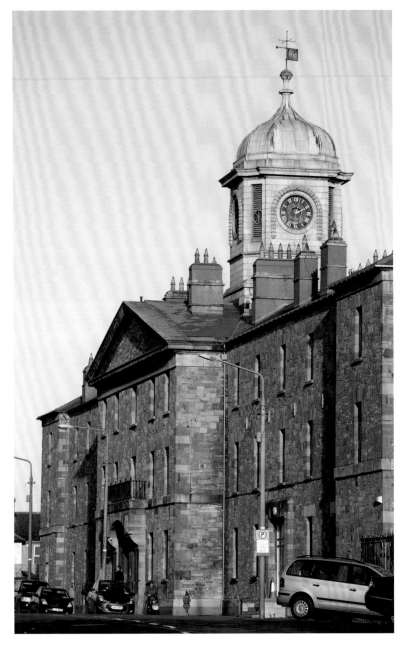

(fig. 56)
RICHMOND PENITENTIARY
(St Brendan's Hospital)
Grangegorman Lower
(1816)

Francis Johnston's penitentiary was given a sober appearance, as befitted such an institution. It once had a five-sided arrangement of buildings to the rear. In 1897 it was incorporated into the Richmond District Lunatic Asylum.

Staircase.

An institutional complex was developed in stages around Grangegorman, on extensive lands belonging to the Monck estate, which had escaped development in the eighteenth century. It shared a site with the House of Industry (1776), which became the North Dublin Union Workhouse in 1841. Francis Johnston designed the Richmond General Penitentiary and the Richmond Lunatic Asylum, both completed in 1815-16 *(fig. 56)*.

(fig. 57)
ST BRENDAN'S HOSPITAL
Fitzwilliam Place North/Morningstar Avenue
(1810)

One of the large blocks, designed by Francis Johnston, that formed part of the large mental hospital complex at Grangegorman.

Coat of arms of the Duke of Richmond, sculpted by Robert Stewart in 1814.

(fig. 58)
ST LAURENCE'S CHAPEL
St Brendan's Hospital Grangegorman Lower
(1849-51)

The Catholic chapel at Grangegorman, designed by Murray and Denny, is very typical of institutional chapels of the mid-nineteenth century.

Despite diverse functions, the design of these buildings shared an architectural strategy that promoted the controlled surveillance of patients and inmates within contained external spaces. Additional land was subsequently acquired to the west to facilitate the construction of St Brendan's Hospital in 1854 *(figs. 57-9)*. Parts of these buildings remain and the site is currently undergoing regeneration works to accommodate the Dublin Institute of Technology campus.

Comical human faces adorn the stops to the hood-moulding of the porch.

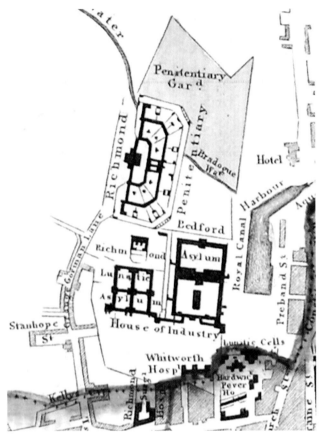

**RICHMOND
PENITENTIARY/RICHMOND
ASYLUM/HOUSE OF INDUSTRY**

Cooke's Royal Map of Dublin was published to coincide with the visit of King George IV to Ireland in August 1821. The excerpt depicts the institutional grouping at Grangegorman. The House of Industry became known as the North Dublin Union workhouse.

Courtesy of National Library of Ireland

(fig. 59)
ST BRENDAN'S HOSPITAL
Grangegorman Lower
(c.1780)

This gateway was moved to the main entrance of the hospital about 1940 from Santry Court, an important early eighteenth-century house north of the city. It displays good decorative stonework and exuberant wrought ironwork.

(fig. 60)
**CENTRAL MODEL
SCHOOLS**
Department of Education
Marlborough
Street/Deverell Place
(1858)

Frederick Darley's model
school has been
compared to an Italianate
railway station. Its scale,
detailing and contrasting
materials give it an
appealing appearance.

(fig. 62)
CLOCKTOWER BUILDING
Department of Education
Marlborough Street
(1838)

Owen also designed the
Infant Model School,
where 300 children were
taught. The dome
replaces an original
lantern.

(fig. 61)
**DEPARTMENT OF
EDUCATION**
Marlborough Street
(1835)

Jacob Owen replicated
the Tyrone mansion of
1740 when laying out his
institutional complex for
the Commissioners of
National Education.

Tyrone House, fronting onto Marlborough Street, was acquired by the Commissioners of National Education in 1835 with the intention of creating an institutional set-piece. In addition to his remodelling of Richard Castle's mansion, Jacob Owen composed the National Model Schools complex, a formal arrangement of educational buildings within landscaped grounds, to serve as an exemplar for teaching facilities nationally *(fig. 60)*. It is currently occupied by its successor, the Department of Education. The site includes a matching replica of Tyrone House to the north of the original, and the handsome centrally placed Clocktower Building, formerly the Infant Model School, which serves as a backdrop to the composition *(figs. 61-2)*.

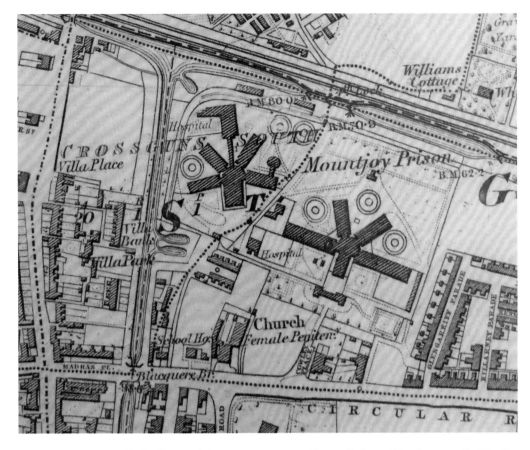

(fig. 63)
MOUNTJOY PRISON
North Circular Road
(1847-50)

Ireland's most famous
prison was designed
by Joshua Jebb and
modelled on London's
Pentonville Prison. It
has a gatehouse
fronting a radial
arrangement of

blocks, all surrounded
by high walls. A
second radial
complex to the
northwest was built
as a female prison
and now houses St
Patrick's Institution
for young offenders.

*Reproduced with the
permission of the
Board of Trinity
College Dublin*

The push for social reform resulted in the
construction of a number of prisons, the largest
of these being Mountjoy Prison, designed by
Joshua Jebb in 1850 on a site between the
North Circular Road and the Royal Canal. The
plan of the complex was based on the
Victorian radial prison model and was
influenced by Jebb's work on Pentonville
Prison in London (1842) *(fig. 63)*. The design
of Arbour Hill Prison, completed in 1848, is
attributed to Richard Cuming and the Royal
Engineers. They were also responsible for the

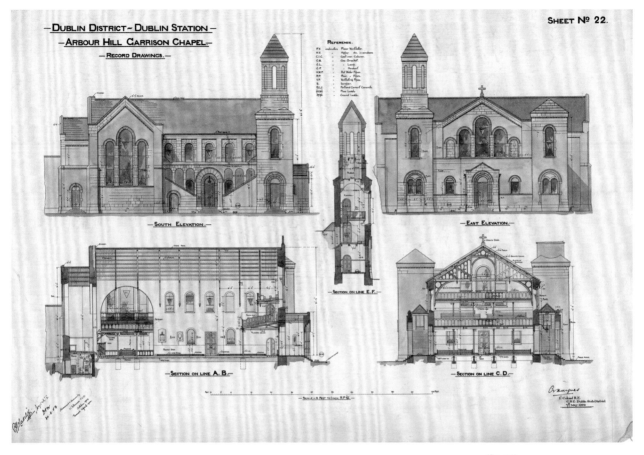

delightful Church of the Sacred Heart, originally the garrison chapel associated with the Arbour Hill barracks *(fig. 64)*. The finely crafted calp limestone structure features carved granite detailing and a stained-glass window by Earley and Co., dated 1925, commemorating those who died fighting for Irish Independence. Pairs of arcaded stairs to the north and south elevations span between the transept and square corner towers, allowing access to the upper galleries.

(fig. 64)
CHURCH OF THE SACRED HEART
Arbour Hill
(1848)

The former garrison church at Arbour Hill Detention Barracks was designed by Richard Cuming of the Royal Engineers and based on the Scotch Church in Bow Street, London. It became the official church of the Irish defence forces in 1997. Adjoining it is the burial place of the executed signatories of the 1916 Proclamation of Independence.

Courtesy of Military Archives

The site for Gardiner's proposed Royal Circus, at the west end of Eccles Street, remained undeveloped for almost a century while construction flourished on neighbouring plots. In 1861, the Mater Hospital was built on the site by the Sisters of Mercy and envisaged as a refuge for the poor. It was designed by John Bourke, has been extended several times, and is now one of the city's major general hospitals *(fig. 65)*.

(fig. 65)
MATER MISERICORDIAE HOSPITAL
Eccles Street
(1855-61)

This major Dublin hospital was built on land originally allocated for the building of the Royal Circus. John Bourke's monumental edifice is set off by its large entrance portico.

(fig. 66)
NORTH CITY FLOUR MILLS
(formerly Mallet's Iron Mill)
Cross Guns Quay
(c.1840)

A large five-storey mill, now
apartments, beside the
Royal Canal at
Phibsborough.

**BLESSINGTON
STREET BASIN**
(1810)

The canal basin at the
west end of
Blessington Street and
the now-infilled canal
branch line to
Broadstone Harbour
(bottom left) are now
part of a public park.

*Reproduced with the
permission of the
Board of Trinity College
Dublin*

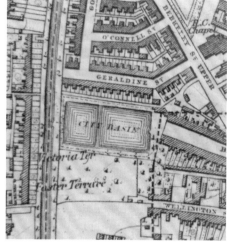

Perhaps the most significant developments to materialise during the century were the infrastructural projects which transformed the cityscape and encouraged economic growth. A site adjacent to the proposed Royal Circus was earmarked for a city reservoir and in 1810 the Blessington Basin was built. Its water supply came via a connecting spur to Royal Canal Harbour. This extension of the canal was filled in to form an urban park in 1927.

The completion of the canal and basin ensured a clean water supply for the north city via a mains system. The canal and the consolidation of the eastern docklands, combined with the arrival of the railway network in the mid-century, did much to promote industry and commerce in the city, particularly milling, brewing and distilling *(fig. 66).*

(fig. 67)
STACK A
George's Dock/Custom
House Quay
(c.1820)

This former tobacco warehouse is a vast, low building 145m long and almost 50m wide. It was designed by John Rennie in the manner of similar structures at the London docks. The largest and finest industrial interior in the Dublin Docklands, it accommodated a huge banquet in 1856 to honour soldiers returning from the Crimean War.

The former masonry river
frontage was given a
glass façade as part of
the renovations in 2004.

The eminent Scottish engineer, John Rennie, employed as a consultant to the Royal Canal Company, was instrumental in the development of the docklands. He was responsible for Custom House Dock, George's Dock and Revenue Dock along the north quays, in addition to a series of industrial warehouses. His Tobacco Warehouse (Stack A) on Custom House Quay is particularly noteworthy and testament to his skills as a designer. Constituting the largest interior space in the city during the nineteenth century, this elegant cast-iron and masonry warehouse sits above a brick and stone-vaulted basement *(fig. 67)*. A recent restoration has retained its material and structural integrity.

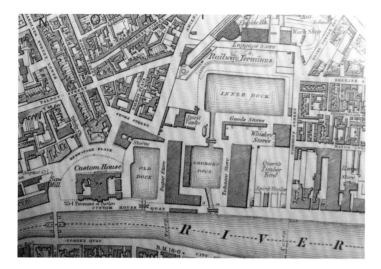

LOADING CRANE
George's Dock
(Late 19th century)

One of the few remnants
of industrial heritage
interest in the old docks.

CUSTOM HOUSE DOCKS
Custom House Quay,
George's Dock, Commons
Street
(1792-1824)

An interesting series of
docks close by the
Custom House. The
oldest, 'Old Dock' was
built in 1792-7 but
infilled in 1927. George's
Dock dates to 1821 and
the Inner (or Revenue)
Dock was erected three
years later. The oldest
two were designed by
John Rennie, who also
designed the huge
Tobacco Warehouse
(Stack A).

*Reproduced with the
permission of the Board of
Trinity College Dublin*

GEORGE'S DOCK

Five railway stations were constructed in the
city between 1833 and 1859. On the north side
are Amiens Street (now Connolly) Station, the
terminus of the Great Northern Railway, and
Broadstone Station, the terminus of the
Midland Great Western Railway. The former
was strategically located close to the Custom
House and the docklands. Built in 1846 to the
designs of John Macneill and William Deane
Butler, the elaborate Italianate façade features a
central campanile and terminates the vista
along Talbot Street *(figs. 68-9)*. This tower is
echoed in John Lanyon's Great Northern
Railway Headquarters, which was constructed
on an adjacent site in 1876 *(fig. 70)*. An
accomplished composition in red brick, with
sandstone detailing, the grandeur of the façade
complements the massing and scale of the
station.

(fig. 68)
CONNOLLY STATION
Amiens Street
(1844-6)

John Macneill and
William Deane Butler's
railway station
terminates the vista
along North Earl and
Talbot streets. Its
campanile is matched
by that of the Great
Northern Railway
(GNR) headquarters to
the north.

(fig. 69)
CONNOLLY STATION
Amiens Street
(1844-6, remodelled
1884)

One of the train sheds,
with typical brick
arcading and a light
roof supported on
cast-iron columns.

(fig. 70)
IARNRÓD ÉIREANN
Amiens Street/Sheriff
Street Lower
(1879)

John Lanyon's
headquarters for the
GNR echoes some of
the features of the
railway station, with a
campanile and
rusticated quoins,
although the sandstone
and red brick are a
striking contrast to the
ashlar granite walls of
the station.

Exuberant treatment to
the entrance porch of
the offices, with a river
god and the logo of
the Great Northern
Railway company.

IARNRÓD ÉIREANN

(fig. 71)
**BROADSTONE
RAILWAY STATION**
(The Director's House)

This neo-Egyptian-style
building accommodated
the offices of the
Midland and Great
Western Railway. The
station was closed in
1937 and converted to
a bus garage.

*Courtesy of Irish
Architectural Archive*

In 1845 the Midland Great Western Railway
Company acquired the Royal Canal, with the
intention of laying the railway along its line
and, in time, replacing it. A branch of the
canal terminated at Broadstone Harbour and a
site to the north was selected for the train
station. John Skipton Mulvany's station,
regarded as one of his masterworks, was
completed in 1850, perched on high ground
overlooking the harbour. Known as the
'Director's House', this commanding structure
of Ballyknockan granite, in a neo-Egyptian
style, was used as offices for the company
(fig. 71). Passengers entered the station proper
through portals at the side. The complex,
which presents an impressive Ionic colonnaded

Passengers entered the station from
both sides of the building. This
Ionic colonnade was added as an
entrance for cabs.

(fig. 72)
GREAT WESTERN SQUARE
(1884)

To the north of Broadstone Station is a pleasant square of houses built by the railway company for its workers.

screen, added in 1861 by George Wilkinson to the east elevation of the train shed, has not been in use as a public railway station since 1937, but its placement proved pivotal in the development of neighbouring sites. Associated buildings, including engineering workshops and guesthouses were constructed to serve the transport hub. Terraced two-storey red brick houses were built for the railway employees on Great Western Square, to the north of the station in 1884 *(fig. 72)*.

LONDON AND NORTH-WESTERN RAILWAY HOTEL (former)
58-9 North Wall Quay
(c.1885)

Now used as offices by CIÉ, this red brick hotel was built to complement the now-demolished North Wall Railway Station that stood immediately to the west. It has fine terracotta details and cast-iron railings.

LOOP LINE RAILWAY BRIDGE (Liffey Viaduct)
(1889-91)

The Loop Line Railway, connecting Connolly and Pearse stations, visually divorced the city from the Custom House and sea, but in acknowledgement, parts of the structure were clad with Portland stone classical details.

(fig. 73)
THE FIVE LAMPS
Amiens Street/North Strand Road
(c.1880)

This combined drinking fountain and lamp standard is a city landmark, erected to the memory of General Henry Hall, who died in 1875.

Nearby, the Five Lamps marks the junction of Amiens Street and North Strand. The provision of this cast-iron lamp standard and drinking fountain, dating from 1880, was an attempt to ease the slum conditions in the district by providing clean drinking water for those lacking access to such a fundamental facility *(fig. 73)*.

14 RICHMOND STREET NORTH

26 SHERRARD STREET UPPER

85 AMIENS STREET

12 DALYMOUNT
North Circular Road
(c.1895)

19 GARDINER PLACE

The city has an extensive heritage of finely wrought and cast ironwork. This is to be seen in the treatment of balconies, boundaries of areas and gardens, and coal-hole covers.

**26 MOUNTJOY
SQUARE EAST**

ST PETER'S CHURCH
North Circular Road

73 CABRA ROAD

**17 MOUNTJOY
SQUARE EAST**

63 CABRA ROAD

(Fig. 74)
**WELLINGTON
TESTIMONIAL**
Phoenix Park
(1817-20, 1857-61)

One of the great
landmarks of Dublin,
on the western
approach, but also
closing the vista
along the Liffey
quays, is the huge
granite obelisk to the
Duke of Wellington.
All four faces bear the
names of his key
victories, the lettering
reputedly cast from
the melting down of
captured cannons.

WELLINGTON TESTIMONIAL

The plaque on the east face reads: 'Asia and Europe, saved by thee, proclaim / Invincible in war thy deathless name, / Now round thy brow the civic oak we twine / That every earthly glory may be thine'.

WELLINGTON TESTIMONIAL

The original unexecuted proposal, showing statuary at the base.

Courtesy of Royal Institute of British Architects Library Drawings Collection

Allegorical depiction by John Hogan of Wellington accepting the civic crown from Britannia, and presenting the scroll of freedom to Hibernia.

The inherited system of roads and urban spaces was consolidated in the latter half of the century. North Circular Road, which circumscribes the north city, spanning from the docklands in the east to Phoenix Park in the west, was laid out in the 1780s, although its eastern end, Seville Place, was not completed until the middle of the nineteenth century.

Phoenix Park remains a significant element in the city plan. Following a period of neglect, it was subject to considerable change and improvement in the early nineteenth century. The Wellington Testimonial, designed by Robert Smirke, was erected in 1820, though sculptural works to the pedestal were not completed until 1861 *(fig. 74)*. A masonry

(fig. 75)
RUSTIC GATE LODGE
Dublin Zoo
Phoenix Park
(1833)

The Rustic Gate Lodge, marking the entrance to Dublin Zoo, was designed by William Deane Butler. It features a thatched roof and original leaded windows.

obelisk sixty-seven metres high, faced in granite ashlar, and set on axis with the west end of the North Circular Road, it was conceived in 1813, two years before the Duke of Wellington's final victory over Napoleon at Waterloo, and the foundation was laid on the second anniversary of that battle.

In 1832, the English architect Decimus Burton was commissioned to devise a master plan for the park. This ambitious project involved the reconstruction of the boundary walls, a reconfiguration of the road network and the provision of new gate lodges. Internal boundaries were removed and strategic landscaping introduced to realign routes and emphasize vistas. The Royal Dublin Zoological Society opened their renowned zoo in the park in 1830 and the entrance was flanked by an engaging half-timbered gate lodge, designed by William Deane Butler in 1833 *(fig. 75)*.

A series of gate lodges was constructed in the park, the majority by Burton, but others attributed to Jacob Owen, who was architect to the Board of Works (now the Office of Public Works) *(figs. 76-9)*. These finely detailed buildings exhibit diverse architectural styles and materials.

(fig. 76)
**CHAPELIZOD GATE
LODGE**
Phoenix Park
(c.1830)

A number of gate
lodges were built or
remodelled within
Phoenix Park in the
1830s as part of
Decimus Burton's
ambitious master plan.

(fig. 77)
**ISLANDBRIDGE GATE
LODGE**
Phoenix Park
(c.1840)

(fig. 79)
WHITE'S LODGE
Phoenix Park
(c.1905)

(fig. 78)
**BESSBORO GATE
LODGE**
Phoenix Park
(c.1847)

The gateways and railings along the boundary of the park have decorative cast-ironwork of a very high standard *(figs. 80-1)*. In 1860 the Board took over the management of the park and effected further improvements. In 1929 the Phoenix Column of 1747 was relocated near the entrance of Áras an Uachtaráin, but has since been reinstated to its original position on Chesterfield Avenue.

(fig. 80)
CASTLEKNOCK GATE
Phoenix Park
(c.1834)

Exemplary cast ironwork by J&C McGloughlin is evident in the gates and railings along the park's boundary.

(fig. 81)
**NORTH CIRCULAR
ROAD GATE**
Phoenix Park
(c.1905)

McKee (formerly Marlborough) Barracks was constructed in 1893 on Blackhorse Avenue, just northeast of the park.

A decorative red brick complex with tiled roofs, it was designed by Robert Barlie and the Royal Engineers to accommodate cavalry units *(fig. 82)*. The Officers' Mess has a seven-bay centrepiece flanked by recessed seven-bay wings terminating in three-bay pavilions. It and several other buildings have fine terracotta detailing and distinctive, steeply pitched roofs punctuated by dormer windows and decorative brick chimneystacks.

(fig. 82)
McKEE BARRACKS
Blackhorse Avenue
(1893)

McKee (formerly Marlborough) Barracks was built by the Royal Engineers. It is an imposing Victorian red brick military structure designed to house cavalry units.

Courtesy of Lagan Building Solutions Ltd.

STABLE BLOCK

STABLE BLOCK

NON-COMMISSIONED OFFICERS' MESS

1-15 SHERRARD STREET LOWER
(c.1830)

2-16 CHARLEVILLE ROAD
(c.1885)

GERALDINE STREET
(c.1875)

1-16 DALYMOUNT
(c.1895)

The establishment of the canal and rail network, and a growing class of skilled artisans and clerks, generated a profusion of new streets around Broadstone and North Circular Road. Reflecting the status of the occupants, the houses on these streets ranged from rows of modest single-storey cottages to terraces of three storeys over raised basements.

Despite this high-quality housing, the majority of the city's population lived in sub-standard, slum accommodation. While commerce thrived, acute levels of poverty were a reality for most city dwellers, many of whom had moved from back lane cottages and mud cabins to the Georgian terraces of the north city. In the absence of basic infrastructure and

(fig. 83)
TEMPLE BUILDINGS
Dominick Street
Upper
(1878)

Built by the Dublin
Artisan Dwellings
Company (DADCo),
Temple Buildings was
inspired by British
housing models. The
seven blocks are
composed in yellow
brick and are stepped
to respond to the
topography of the
street. DADCo,
founded in 1876,
erected some 3,600
dwellings.

sanitation, Dublin's housing situation reached a crisis point, exacerbated by the arrival in the city of large numbers of the rural population during the years of the Great Famine. Griffith's Valuation, carried out in Dublin in 1848-64, provides a record of the extreme poverty and dire living conditions in the city. Conversely, the upsurge in commercial and economic activity in the 1860s, brought about by the introduction of the railway and consolidation of the docklands, led to the establishment of affluent housing areas outside the city core, in suburbs such as Drumcondra, Clontarf, Rathmines and Donnybrook.

In 1866 bye-laws were introduced that specified minimum standards of housing and sanitation. Despite the threat of fines, breaches of these standards were commonplace.

However, in 1876, the Dublin Artisans' Dwellings Company (DADCo) was established to begin addressing the shortfall in housing. With Edward Guinness as chairman, and assistance from Dublin Corporation in the acquisition of sites and supportive loans, DADCo oversaw the construction of up to 3,600 new dwellings across the city. The early DADCo schemes drew inspiration from contemporary British housing models and took the form of large tenement blocks, such as Temple Buildings (1878) on Upper Dominick Street, which reference the scale and materiality of Georgian terraces *(fig. 83)*. Designed by T.N. Deane & Son, these imposing four-storey brown brick blocks exhibit a minimal Gothic style, with pointed entrance openings and decorative red brick dressings.

Later DADCo housing projects adapted the terraced cottage model. In Stoneybatter, a densely woven grid of streets was built between 1879 and 1908, lined with terraces of single and two-storey houses. The yellow brick façades feature decorative red brick embellishments and simple but high-quality details, such as dentillated brick cornicing and integrated boot-scrapers *(fig. 84)*. The architect, Charles Ashworth, was responsible for several of the DADCo schemes, devising five plan variations, having two to four bedrooms.

Public outcry at a lack of housing for the poorer population prompted the 1885 Housing Inquiry. The relatively high rents associated with DADCo dwellings meant that they were typically occupied by skilled workers and not accessible to less fortunate citizens. Dublin Corporation was under pressure to alleviate the crisis and so devised a number of social housing strategies. The first Dublin Corporation public housing projects were based on the Scottish tenement model, with communal staircases and one and two-bedroom flats, sharing similarities with the early DADCo blocks. One such development was Ellis Court and the adjacent block on Benburb Street, a scheme which dates from 1885 and was designed by D.J. Freeman, the City Architect *(fig. 85)*. These robust red brick edifices display blue brick embellishments and granite plinths, feature shopfronts, and have decorative breakfronts announcing the stairwells.

Public housing in the 1890s reverted to the terraced cottage model, each dwelling having its own plot and modest rear yard, examples

(fig. 84)
STONEYBATTER
(1879-1908)

A typical DADCo house in this area of brick-built mass housing.

of which can be seen in St Joseph's Place off Dorset Street *(fig. 86)*. These red brick terraces with segmental-headed openings and pitched slate roofs formed a typology that endured throughout the city into the early twentieth century. Another popular typology, on a more generous scale, was the red brick split-level terraced house, a single-storey elevation concealing two storeys to the rear, often presenting a bay window to the street and giving a sense of formality and grandeur to what were modest houses.

(fig. 85)
73-74 BENBURB STREET
(1885)

An early example of a purpose-built apartment block in Dublin, this red brick housing scheme and the adjacent Ellis Court development were based on the Scottish tenement model and designed by City Architect, Daniel J. Freeman. The elevations feature polychromatic brickwork, with decorative cast-iron panels to the parapet providing visual and textural contrast.

(fig. 86)
ST JOSEPH'S PLACE
(1890s)

These terraced red brick houses are typical of Dublin Corporation projects in the 1890s, when tenement blocks were replaced by the cottage model, a typology that endured well into the twentieth century.

(fig. 87)
DUBLIN WRITERS MUSEUM
18 Parnell Square
(c.1765, remodelled c.1890)

The extensive remodelling of Georgian residences was a common practice across the city towards the end of the nineteenth century. This house was adapted in the closing years of the century for the Jameson family.

In the absence of newly constructed mansions, some eighteenth-century dwellings were remodelled in the late nineteenth century to cater for the demand for grander residences. Such interventions are evident in houses throughout the north city, notably 18 Parnell Square (currently the Dublin Writers Museum) and, on a larger scale, Farmleigh, a relatively modest Georgian house that was extended and renovated by James Franklin Fuller in 1884 to provide a home for Edward Guinness *(figs. 87-8)*.

DUBLIN WRITERS MUSEUM

DUBLIN WRITERS MUSEUM

(fig. 88)
FARMLEIGH HOUSE
White's Road
(Late 18th century,
extended 1881-4)

Farmleigh was
purchased by Edward
Cecil Guinness in
1873 on his marriage
to Adelaide Guinness.

*Courtesy of Office of
Public Works*

(fig. 89)
78-84 CAPEL STREET
(1820s)

A terrace laid out by the Wide Streets Commissioners, with timber shopfronts at street level and residential quarters above. The street was home to many tradespeople who often resided in and operated out of the same building. The shopfront has adjoining doorways, one giving access to the shop and the other to accommodation above.

The notion of 'living over the shop' had been mooted by the Wide Streets Commissioners in their proposals for Cavendish Row in 1787. Several decades later, changing work practices and the new living arrangements of the rising 'middle class' firmly established this new typology, an example of which can be found in Capel Street, then emerging as a thriving commercial hub. 78-84 Capel Street is a modest terrace of residential buildings laid out by the Commissioners in the 1820s, designed with commercial units to the ground floor *(fig. 89)*. Their decorative timber shopfronts address the street and timber Wyatt or tripartite windows enhance the plain brick façades.

(fig. 90)
114-116 CAPEL STREET
(1871, altered 1879)

The elaborate façade reflects the original use of this building as a showroom for James Kerr, manufacturer of Belleek china. It also served as the headquarters of the United Trades Council and Labour League in 1935.

114-116 CAPEL STREET

The main entrance doors feature pretty cast-iron grilles to the upper panels.

As the century progressed and the demand for commercial premises grew, Georgian dwellings were commonly adapted to accommodate these new functions. Eighteenth-century structures were remodelled to incorporate elaborate shopfronts, pub-fronts and reconfigured interiors. Many of these interventions are illustrated in Henry Shaw's Dublin City Directory for 1850. The showrooms at 114-116 Capel Street were built in 1871 by John McCurdy to display Kerr's Belleek china, but were remodelled only eight years later by Albert E. Murray for the Dublin Coffee Tavern Company. The animated ground floor façade comprises a five-bay stuccoed blind arcade punctuated by Doric half-columns, concealing a richly decorated salon *(fig. 90)*.

Many ornate pub-fronts appeared in the late nineteenth century, commonly executed in timber and stone with decorative brickwork to the upper levels. The façades featured embellishments such as carved stone capitals and gargoyles, testament to the skill and craftsmanship of stonemasons at that time, and a penchant for Gothic Revival motifs.

(fig. 91)
AURORA BAR & GRILL
72-73 Dorset Street
(c.1880)

This prominently positioned public house exhibits a handsome front on a largely Georgian streetscape, comprising a series of deep moulded arches on polished pink granite engaged columns with stiff-leaf capitals.

(fig. 92)
L. MULLIGAN
18 Stoneybatter
(c.1800, shopfront c.1880]

The Aurora Bar on Dorset Street, dating from 1880, displays a similar arcaded Victorian pub-front, forming a stark contrast with the plain red brick composition of the upper floors *(fig. 91)*. The elevation treatments to Mulligan's and the Glimmer Man pubs in Stoneybatter, Jack Nealon's on Capel Street and The Hut on Phibsborough Road, exhibit typically Victorian detailing *(figs. 92-5)*.

(fig. 93)
THE GLIMMERMAN
14-15 Stoneybatter
(c.1880)

(fig. 94)
JACK NEALON
165-166 Capel Street/Little
Strand Street
(1867)

(fig. 95)
MOHAN'S/THE HUT
159 Phibsborough Road
(c.1898)

(fig. 96)
AXA (formerly Beakey &
Co. Warehouse)
Wolfe Tone Street/12-13
Mary Street
(1863)

Designed by William
Murray, the warehouse
for Beakey & Co.
originally featured a
top-lit internal court,
but was adapted to
incorporate a cinema in
1912. Vermiculated
friezes and decorative
roundels enliven the
stuccoed façade.

Elsewhere, distinctive Victorian flourishes appeared on eighteenth-century façades, such as the stucco panels that decorate 144 Parnell Street.

The former warehouse for Beakey & Co. cabinet-makers, now AXA Insurance, stands at the junction of Mary Street and Wolfe Tone Street *(fig. 96)*. The building, which was designed by William Murray in 1863, features a flamboyant stuccoed façade and was adapted to house the Mary Street Picture House in the early twentieth century.

(fig. 97)
PENNEYS *(formerly Todd Burns & Co.)*
45-47 Mary Street
(1902-5)

Built by W.M. Mitchell for Todd Burns & Co, this commanding red brick edifice is crowned by an ornate copper dome over a central pedimented bay, dominating the corner of Mary Street and Jervis Street.

Also on Mary Street is W.M. Mitchell's red brick department store for Todd Burns & Co, currently occupied by Penneys *(fig. 97)*. A recent extension to the store was built on the site of the former Volta Electric Theatre, Dublin's first cinema, established by James Joyce in 1909.

Arnotts Department Store was designed by G.P. Beater in 1894 on Henry Street, another important commercial thoroughfare *(fig. 98)*. One of only two Victorian buildings on the street to survive destruction in the 1916 Rising, Arnotts is a wonderful example of decorative Victorian architecture. The façade is composed of red brick, pink granite and terracotta, and features Gothic elements and a central five-stage campanile.

(fig. 99)
STANDARD LIFE ASSURANCE CO.
(former)
65-66 O'Connell Street Upper
(1861-3)

John Steell's 'The Wise and Foolish Virgins' decorates the tympanum, echoing a design used at the company's head office in Edinburgh.

The economic upsurge of the 1860s brought with it a wealth of distinguished bank and insurance buildings, with a particular concentration around College Green and Dame Street, but with some examples north of the Liffey. The Scottish architect, David Bryce, was responsible for the Standard Life Assurance Company at 65-66 Upper O'Connell Street, completed in 1863 *(fig. 99)*. The ashlar sandstone portico displays a finely executed carved tympanum depicting 'The Wise and Foolish Virgins' sculpted by John Steell. Close by is the former Colonial Insurance Company premises, a mid-eighteenth-century building refaced in 1863 to designs by W.G. Murray, with an arcade theme *(fig. 100)*.

(fig. 98)
ARNOTTS
7-15 Henry Street
(1894)

Arnotts Department Store represents a characteristically Victorian design, invigorating the street with a lively façade featuring elements of past architectural styles. The central campanile and oriel window, along with the bold use of terracotta and limestone, are of particular interest.

(fig. 100)
DUBLIN BUS
60 Upper O'Connell Street
(c.1750, remodelled 1863)

This elegant red brick building features carved sandstone courses and mouldings, and a painted stucco ground floor.

Two significant examples of commercial and industrial architecture were embedded in the infrastructure of the city in the closing decade of the century. The construction of the sprawling Jameson Distillery in Smithfield in 1895 was testament to the prominence of brewing and distilling as primary industries in Ireland. Elements of the original complex remain, notably the great red brick screen wall and the boiler-house chimney stack, which dominate the square *(fig. 101)*. Remnants of the calp limestone warehouses survive on adjacent streets.

The City Fruit & Vegetable Market was designed by Parke Neville, City Engineer, and built on Mary's Lane in 1892, in what was historically a market quarter. An exemplary model of Victorian public architecture, spanning a full urban block, the extensive red brick and terracotta dressed market building features an elaborate internal ironwork structure *(fig. 102)*. The decorative façade features pretty terracotta details depicting the produce for sale within.

(fig. 101)
JAMESON'S DISTILLERY (former)
Smithfield
(1895, altered 1998)

Laid out in 1665, Smithfield Market was intended to be the centrepiece of a proposed new quarter in the northwest of the city. Today it has new residential blocks and arts facilities. The distillery chimney stack and surviving screen wall are reminders of a once-thriving industry.

(fig. 102)
CITY FRUIT AND VEGETABLE MARKET
Chancery Street/St Michan's Street (1892)

The expansive City Fruit and Vegetable Market displays exquisite terracotta detailing externally and encloses an elaborate ironwork structure. Ornate iron tympana by McGloughlin & Son ensure it is well ventilated.

The Twentieth Century

(fig. 103)
**RICHMOND
HOSPITAL** (former)
Brunswick Street North
(1895-1900)

On its opening *The
Irish Times* (April 22
1901) listed some of
the Richmond
Hospital's modern
features: 'it's
"practically fireproof",
boasts modern
ventilation throughout
and warmed filtered
air for the theatres'.

The nineteenth century had brought about
extensive change in the city and yet the
dominating street framework as the new
century opened was that of the Georgian era.

There was a continuation of styles from the
previous century in such major projects as the
Richmond Hospital of 1900 and St Peter's
Church, Phibsborough. 'The Richmond',
designed by Carroll & Batchelor, is an
exuberant U-plan edifice in brick. It has
balconies and colonnaded verandas for
convalescent patients to the forward
projections, and ogee domes to turrets at the
corners. The brick and terracotta detailing is of
a particularly high quality. The building was
later a courthouse and is now occupied by
the Irish Nurses and Midwives Organisation

(fig. 104)
ST PETER'S CHURCH
North Circular Road/Cabra Road
Phibsborough
(1858-1911)

The siting and scale of St Peter's, illustrated here in the *Irish Builder*, make it a landmark. Its High Cross (1856) is an early example of Celtic Revival in Dublin. The building contains works by Ireland's most important stained-glass artist, Harry Clarke (who had his studio on North Frederick Street). 'The Adoration of the Sacred Heart' was made in 1919; the twin-light windows of 1924 are abstract in design, contrasting with Clarke's usual figurative approach.

Drawing courtesy of Irish Architectural Archive

(fig. 103). The earliest part of the church at Phibsborough dates to the 1820s, but the building was altered and extended in 1850 by John Bourke, and again in 1858-68 by Weightman, Hadfield and Goldie. In 1903-11 Ashlin and Coleman substantially re-edified the building, which has a prominent spire and stonework and detailing of a very high order *(fig. 104)*. There is also a renowned collection of stained-glass windows, including works by Harry Clarke, among them his Adoration of the Sacred Heart (1919).

(fig. 105)
**DUBLIN INSTITUTE
OF TECHNOLOGY**
Bolton Street/King's
Inns Street
(1909-11)

The classical detailing
of the building and
its extension reflect a
certain conservatism
of taste.

C.J. McCarthy's Dublin Institute of Technology (1909-11) on Bolton Street is a thirteen-bay classically composed building with a pedimented breakfront entrance. It was extended to the northeast in 1961, through the addition of eight bays that replicated the appearance of the original façade *(fig. 105)*.

The monument to Charles Stewart Parnell, terminating the vista northwards along O'Connell Street, was unveiled in 1911, although dated 1906. It was designed by the Irish-American sculptor Augustus Saint-Gaudens, assisted by the architects Henry Bacon and George Sheridan. The gilt lettering reads: 'No Man has a right to fix the boundary to the march of a nation. No man has a right to say to his country "Thus far shalt thou go and no further"' *(fig. 106)*.

(fig. 106)
PARNELL MONUMENT
O'Connell Street
(1906)

The erection of this
monument to Charles
Stewart Parnell on Dublin's
principal thoroughfare was
an important statement of a
re-emerging national
movement. There are
attractive cast-iron air vents
to the foreground.

**PARNELL
MONUMENT**

Bronze statue by
Augustus Saint-
Gaudens.

THE LAST HOUR OF THE NIGHT

Harry Clarke's stunning image, the frontispiece to Patrick Abercrombie's *Dublin of the Future: The New Town Plan* (1922) shows a spectre hanging over the city, with the GPO, Custom House and Four Courts in flames, and its Georgian houses supported by raking shores.

Courtesy of Irish Architectural Archive

The last hour of the Night.

Though slums had infiltrated the inner city streets, the eighteenth-century fabric was remarkably intact and remained so until the 1960s. However, the extreme levels of poverty sparked considerable debate in matters of planning and architecture in the early decades of the century. In 1913, the housing reformer E.A. Aston reported that one third of the population of Dublin was living in one-room tenements. The city reputedly had the worst slums in Europe and the ever-worsening housing crisis was brought to a head with the collapse of two tenement properties on Church Street that resulted in the deaths of seven people. This tragedy, and the horrors of everyday life in the tenements, was well documented in contemporary photographs. Public outcry led to an official housing inquiry, the results of which were published in 1914. It reported that over 60,000 people lived in accommodation 'decayed or so badly constructed' that it was unfit and incapable of being rendered fit or was borderline unfit for habitation. The Chief Secretary for Ireland, Augustine Birrell, wrote 'there can be no mistake that the state of things which now exists is horrible and intolerable.'

(fig. 107)
ORMOND SQUARE
(1917-21)

A small Dublin Corporation housing scheme that retains the outline plan of the former Ormond Market. The red brick banding and arches over the doors and windows raise it above the ordinary.

Alternatives to city housing were proposed by two invited British planning consultants, Raymond Unwin and Patrick Geddes who espoused the Garden City ideals popular in England at the time. They analysed Dublin Corporation housing schemes, inspected sites and formulated a report, generally calling for lower densities and garden-suburb type developments. Despite this emergent thinking, the Corporation completed a number of socially innovative city centre housing developments in subsequent years. Among these was Ormond Square, designed by C.J. McCarthy, City Architect (1893-1921), and built between 1917 and 1921 on the site of the former Ormond Market *(fig. 107)*. Comprising traditionally crafted artisans' cottages constructed in yellow brick and roofed in slate, the scheme introduced mixed dwelling types and was centred on a landscaped square, creating a social hub for the local community.

HENRY ST. LOOKING EAST, DUBLIN.

HENRY STREET, 1916

Photograph showing the level of destruction in the immediate vicinity of the GPO. Curiously, Nelson's Pillar appears to be completely untouched.

Image reproduced by kind permission of the estate of Thomas W. Murphy (Dublin City Library and Archive)

A turbulent period in Dublin's history followed, with the 1916 Easter Rising, the War of Independence (1919-21) and the Civil War (1922-3) all taking a heavy toll on the urban fabric, particularly in the north inner city and quaysides. The city authorities embarked on an ambitious rebuilding project during the 1920s under the guidance of Horace O'Rourke, City Architect 1922-45. The opportunity was taken to mark the new state's independence and national identity by renaming several streets including Sackville Street (O'Connell Street) and Rutland Square (Parnell Square).

7-9B ABBEY STREET LOWER (c.1920)

A commercial building, built as part of the reconstruction of the O'Connell Street area, maintaining the vertical emphasis and plot ratios of the earlier buildings.

(fig. 108)
GPO
O'Connell Street
(Rebuilt 1929)

The public hall.
It has beautiful
bronze doors.

The 1920s saw the reconstruction of large sections of the O'Connell Street district and of key public buildings, such as the Custom House, Four Courts and GPO. Dublin Corporation appointed a Reconstruction Committee, and Raymond Unwin was again consulted. Parameters were set out with the intention of allowing individual expression within a coherent design framework. Strict guidelines regarding heights and proportions were imposed to ensure that the character of the streets was retained. So, despite the employment of modern construction techniques and the opportunity to assert a new identity, the architectural expression of this significant phase in Dublin's history was conservative in nature. For the most part, stone classical façades that featured restrained Art Deco detailing, were used as a cladding to reinforced concrete structures. The GPO was extensively rebuilt by T.J. Byrne and J. Fairweather of the Office of Public Works. The new layout featured a central courtyard (being adapted at the time of writing to house a 1916 museum as a centenary project), and a sumptuous neoclassical interior *(fig. 108)*.

(fig. 109)
SAVOY CINEMA
O'Connell Street
(1929)

The Savoy was designed by English architect F.C. Mitchell on the site of the former Granville Hotel. Although its original auditorium, which seated 2,789, is now lost, it is the last historic cinema still in use in the city.

(fig. 110)
CARLTON CINEMA
O'Connell Street
(1937)

An Art Deco façade, in true Hollywood spirit, by architects Robinson & Keefe.

(fig. 111)
CLERYS DEPARTMENT STORE
O'Connell Street
(1918-22)

The design of this iconic department store is now attributed to Robert F Atkinson (1871-1923), who was an assistant at Ashlin & Coleman. He had worked on Selfridges, London, and previously in Chicago.

During this building phase, 'cathedrals' of a new secular culture began to take precedence over religious buildings. In a move reflective of this change, the Savoy Cinema, designed by Charles Mitchell, was built in 1929 on land that had been earmarked for a new Catholic cathedral *(fig. 109)*. The decorative Portland stone frontage of the cinema forms a centrepiece on O'Connell Street. Though an abundance of interior fabric has been lost both the Savoy and the Carlton Cinema opposite, the latter by Robinson & Keefe and built in 1937, are fine representations of Irish cinema architecture *(fig. 110)*. Clerys Department Store, built 1918-22, sadly closed at the time of writing, was rebuilt using the innovative

(fig. 112)
GRESHAM HOTEL
O'Connell Street
(1927)

A stripped classical façade, with
Art Deco influences, was used
for the rebuilding of the hotel
by English architect Robert
Atkinson (1883-1952).

HAMMAM BUILDINGS

Beautiful bronze doors, demonstrating the
quality of materials and detailing used in the
reconstruction of O'Connell Street.

reinforced concrete Hennibique system, the
architect Robert Atkinson drawing his
inspiration from Selfridges of Oxford Street,
London, which was completed in 1909
(fig. 111). The Gresham Hotel, rebuilt in 1927,
has a nine-bay Portland stone façade, its
arcaded ground floor in the Ionic order
disguising a concrete structure *(fig. 112)*. On a
similar scale, Hammam Buildings, completed
in 1925, displays a stripped classical aesthetic
(fig. 113).

(fig. 113)
**HAMMAM
BUILDINGS**
O'Connell Street
(1925)

Attributed to the
Cork architects
Chillingworth &
Levie, this building
derives its name
from the Hammam
Hotel, destroyed in
1922, and which
contained Turkish
baths.

ULSTER BANK
3-4 O'Connell Street
(1923)

Former Hibernian
Bank by James
Hanna, distinguished
by its Palladian
portico in antis, in
line with the façade
rather than in front.

(fig. 114)
**MARLBOROUGH
STREET**
(c.1905)

Historic post boxes
with the royal cipher
and crown are
becoming
increasingly rare. This
example is by
McDowall Steven of
Glasgow.

(fig. 115)
O'CONNELL STREET
(c.1965)

An oval pillar box of
a type first
introduced in London
in 1899, but in use
in Dublin only from
1965.

More subtle changes in the streetscape
include the many fine-quality mass-produced
cast-iron pillar post boxes from the early years
of the Irish Free State, identified by raised
Gaelic lettering *(fig. 114)*. These are
distinguishable from the colonial-era examples
bearing the royal insignia of Victoria or Edward
(fig. 115).

(fig. 116)
INDEPENDENT HOUSE
87-90 Middle Abbey
Street
(1924)

Built on the site of
the offices of the
'Nation' newspaper,
this building was the
most important centre
of the newsprint
industry in Ireland.

The rebuilding programme extended to neighbouring streets and 1924 saw the construction of Independent House on Abbey Street, designed by Donnelly, Moore, Keefe & Robinson Architects *(fig. 116)*. The former newspaper headquarters dominates the streetscape - a neoclassical composition in red brick and Portland stone, featuring a charming Art Deco copper clock projecting from the façade.

(fig. 117)
ST THOMAS'S CHURCH
Cathal Brugha Street
(1931)

A simple but finely detailed church, its exposed brick interior displaying mosaic work by Oppenheimer and stained glass by Catherine O'Brien.

Alterations to the urban structure were modest. Cathal Brugha Street was laid out as an extension of Seán McDermott (formerly Gloucester) Street, but development along the street was piecemeal. Frederick Hicks' Romanesque St Thomas's Church occupies an island site on the street, a 1931 replacement of the nearby eighteenth-century church that was destroyed by fire in 1922 *(fig. 117)*. Robinson & Keefe's Art Deco College of Catering, a reinforced concrete structure clad in brick and granite, followed nearly a decade later *(fig. 118)*.

(fig. 118)
COLLEGE OF CATERING
Cathal Brugha Street/Marlborough Street
(1938-9)

Designed by Robinson & Keefe and built as the College of Domestic Science, its quality reflects the importance placed on education in the early years of Independence. Gabriel Hayes' Three Graces represent Sweeping, Spinning and Sewing – attributes deemed appropriate for the building. The interior is one of the finest of the period in the city, with a rich palette of materials – marble, limestone, steel, terrazzo and timber.

The 1925 Civic Survey further highlighted the housing crisis in Dublin, and in the 1930s and 1940s Dublin Corporation redoubled their efforts towards alleviating the problem. Like many within the corporation, the City Architect, Horace O'Rourke was fixated on the garden suburb ideal as celebrated by Geddes and depicted in Patrick Abercrombie's 1922 plan Dublin of the Future.

As part of the government's resolve to provide 12,000 dwellings annually, plans were advanced for extensive swathes of two-storey 'cottages' in Cabra and Crumlin from the 1930s onwards. However, the argument was made that such suburban ventures would do little to ameliorate the situation for the poorest city dwellers.

Several city centre schemes were initiated to address this demand, under the direction of Herbert Simms, who was appointed Corporation Housing Architect in 1933. He made an extraordinary contribution to Dublin's housing stock, until his premature death in 1948. He oversaw the design and construction of twenty-one housing schemes, many of which were influenced by contemporary Dutch housing typologies. Chancery House is one such example, built by G. & T. Crampton in 1935. Composed in brick and render, featuring rounded corners, over-sailing flat roofs and arched gateways, the scheme draws from works by Michel de Klerk in Amsterdam and J.J.P. Oud in Rotterdam *(fig. 119)*. Henrietta House is another example, this time predominantly brick and with a softer appearance *(fig. 120)*.

ST FINTAN ROAD
Cabra
(Early 1930s)

Local authority housing estates were built on the edge of the city, influenced by the ideas of the Garden City movement. This particular house form is widespread throughout the suburbs of Dublin.

(fig. 119)
CHANCERY HOUSE
Chancery Place
(1935)
The scale and detailing of Simms' designs give them an urban quality unique for twentieth-century housing in the city.

CHANCERY HOUSE

The block is on a U-shaped plan with shared staircases and balcony access provided to each level.

(fig. 120)
HENRIETTA HOUSE
Henrietta Place
(1936)

The detailing was
influenced by the
early twentieth-
century Amsterdam
School municipal
housing schemes.

(fig. 121)
**PHIBSBOROUGH
PUBLIC LIBRARY**
North Circular Road
(1935)

A local public library
built by Dublin
Corporation on a site
that had formed part
of the canal spur to
Broadstone Harbour.

The city authorities were also engaged in the building of libraries. Phibsborough Library was built in 1935 to a design by Robert Lawrie, and was one of four similar facilities erected by the Corporation between 1935 and 1940 *(fig. 121)*.

(fig. 122)
MOUNT CARMEL SCHOOL
King's Inns Street
(1941)

This well-detailed school, by W.H. Byrne & Son, is enlivened by its unusual diamond-patterned brickwork. The plaque over the entrance is by Joseph Hammond.

(fig. 123)
ST LAURENCE O'TOOLE'S CBS SCHOOL
Seville Place
(1936)

The white render and horizontal fenestration are characteristic of early Modernism.

A number of schools were established in the 1930s. W.H. Byrne's Mount Carmel School presents a fetching diamond-patterned brick façade to King's Inns Street *(fig. 122)*. Robinson & Keefe were the architects for St Laurence O'Toole's National School on Seville Place, completed in 1936 *(fig. 123)*. It employs many of the characteristic features of the Modernist style – flat roofs, strong horizontal lines, a curved external staircase and ample use of white render.

(fig. 124)
HENDRONS
Dominick Street
Upper
(1946-59)

Designed by the
Czech engineer,
Vaclav Gunzl (1900-
82), former manager
of the Hendrons
machinery workshop.

R&H HALL
Alexandra Road
(1920-37)

The massive bulk of
this reinforced-
concrete structure is
broken down by its
dentillated cornice
and the framing of
the bays with giant
pilasters.

The Hendron building on Dominick Street also bears influences of International Modernism. Designed by Vaclav Gunzl and constructed between 1946 and 1959, this factory warehouse is a rare surviving example of modernist industrial architecture in the city *(fig. 124)*.

Commissioned by the newly formed national transport authority, Córas Iompair Éireann (CIÉ), Michael Scott's Busáras announced the arrival of Modernism in Ireland *(fig. 125)*. Stylistically the building relates to the work of Swiss-French architect Le Corbusier, most notably the Pavillon Suisse in Paris. Conceived as a bus station and completed in 1953, the finished building incorporated offices for the Department of Social Welfare, a rooftop restaurant, and a newsreel cinema in the basement. Integrated artwork and skilled craft were embraced within the brief, reflecting Scott's collaborative approach to design. This broader interpretation of the scope of architecture allowed the inclusion of colourful hand-crafted mosaics by Patrick Scott, Danish bronze double-glazed windows, ornate ironmongery and bespoke furniture. The sheer virtuosity of the cantilevered corrugated concrete canopy to the concourse is testament to the skills of the Danish engineer, Ove Arup, who went on to collaborate with Scott on numerous projects.

(fig. 125)
BUSÁRAS
Store Street
(1946-53)

The completion of Busáras marked the arrival of full-blown International Modernism in Ireland – remarkable also for its occurrence in a period of post-war shortages and austerity. The wave-like concrete shell roof over the concourse is a structural tour-de-force by the Danish engineer Ove Arup.

Busáras is full of often unnoticed surprises, such as the mosaic tiling to the underside of this high level canopy.

The Garden of Remembrance on Parnell Square was designed by Dáithí Hanly, City Architect (1959-65), following a competition in 1946. Built to commemorate those who died in the struggle for Independence, the garden was completed in 1966, in time for fiftieth anniversary of the 1916 Rising. The centrepiece is a sunken cruciform pool decorated with blue mosaic tiles, depicting a repetitive motif of shields and spears. Oisín Kelly's bronze sculpture, The Children of Lir, was added to the adjacent raised plinth in 1971, providing a focal point within the marble-clad 'apse' *(fig. 126)*.

The mythological Children of Lir, reborn after 900 years imprisoned as swans, symbolising the rebirth of the nation after the struggle for Independence

The depiction of swords and shields in the pool is a reminder of the late prehistoric ritual sacrifice of weapons.

(fig. 126)
GARDEN OF REMEMBRANCE
Parnell Square
(Opened 1966)

The Garden of Remembrance is the most important built legacy of the fiftieth anniversary commemorations of the 1916 Easter Rising.

With the exception of Busáras and Catholic church-related building in the suburbs, there was limited scope for large-scale public projects in the 1950s. This changed in the following decade, when a new confidence emerged, and with it came a new architecture. Several young architects returned to Irish soil having studied and practised in the United States, bringing with them American-style Modernism. Ronnie Tallon, a partner in Michael Scott's practice, worked on designs for the new Abbey Theatre, completed in 1966, replacing the earlier building destroyed in a fire in 1951. Tallon's building comprises a Mies Van der Rohe-inspired brick monolith with clerestory fenestration, to which a two-storey portico was added by McCullough Mulvin Architects in 1991 *(fig. 127)*. Desmond Rea O'Kelly's Liberty Hall was constructed on the north quays in 1964 and, at sixty metres, remains the tallest building in Dublin *(fig. 128)*. A seventeen-storey glazed office block celebrating the functional aesthetic of the International Style, its folded concrete canopy serves as a reference to the nearby Busáras.

However, the establishment of a new architectural identity in the 1960s also saw the demolition of considerable tracts of historic fabric across the north city, partly prompted by the collapse of tenements in 1963 where four lives were tragically lost. The 1970s witnessed further urban decay, neglect and dereliction, where urban design strategies seemed lacking. Buildings of this period typically asserted an independent presence, with radically new materials and of a scale that made little attempt to address their context. There were of course exceptions, one being Robin Walker's PMPA (now AXA) office building on Wolfe

(fig. 127)
ABBEY THEATRE
Marlborough Street
(1966)

The entrance to this monolithic brick box was given emphasis by the later addition of a portico.

(fig. 128)
LIBERTY HALL
Beresford Place
(1965)

Dublin's tallest building, headquarters of the trade union SIPTU, was built on the site of the historic Liberty Hall where the 1916 Proclamation of Independence was printed.

(fig. 129)
AXA
Wolfe Tone Street
(1979)

This finely made building, while respecting its historic context, is clearly of its time. A fairground ride is sandwiched between the reflections of the dome of Penneys store on Mary Street and the tower of St Mary's Church of Ireland church on Wolfe Tone Square.

Tone Street, an infill project completed in 1979 *(fig. 129)*. The rhythm and scale of the carefully crafted façade mimic the composition of the neighbouring structures, while introducing a sleek modernity to the square.

Photographic records from the early 1980s portray a scarred urban landscape, and proposed road-widening plans signalled further ruination, prompting widespread protest. Contemporary debate spurred a reinvention of the role of the architect in civic matters, and practitioners rejected the modernist 'total design' approach to city planning. The year 1986 marked a turning point for Dublin, with the passing of the first Urban Renewal Act, an attempt to engage private developers to actively participate in urban renewal. This legislation signalled the beginnings of a change in attitude to the city's development and paved the way for a new phase in urban history, culminating in Group 91's masterplan for the regeneration of Temple Bar, south of the river, and in the redevelopment of the docklands.

(fig. 130)
JUVENILE COURT
Smithfield
(1987)

Commissioned and
built when Smithfield
was almost in ruins,
this is a statement of
the future potential of
this magnificent
urban space.

The Office of Public Works' Juvenile Court at Smithfield was designed by John Tuomey amidst this transition. Boldly anchoring the corner of the derelict Jameson Distillery complex, the project is illustrative of an attempt to preserve the industrial character of a site that had been destined for demolition *(fig. 130)*. This retention and reworking of existing structures went on to characterise much of O'Donnell + Tuomey's architectural work. In a similar vein, Grafton Architects' infill office building on Ormond Quay was emblematic of this contextual approach to design, comprising the respectful re-use of an historic church façade *(fig. 131)*.

There was also a greater state investment in conservation projects in the 1990s. This involved the refurbishment of significant public buildings, such as the Custom House and Collins Barracks, by the OPW and Gilroy McMahon Architects, the barracks being adapted to house the Decorative Arts & History collection of the National Museum of Ireland.

(fig. 131)
PRESBYTERIAN CHURCH (former)
2-3 Ormond Quay Upper
(1847, 1989)

The church was demolished in 1969, except for the ground level of the façade, which was incorporated into a design for modern offices.

THE ROBERTS HOUSE
Dublin Zoo
(1902)

Designed by L.A. McDonnell in memory of a president of Dublin Zoo, Field Marshal Frederick Roberts, this brick and terracotta building, now used as an aviary, announces its original purpose through the lion mask sculptures to the exterior. The Zoo's breeding programme made it world famous and the famous 'MGM lion' was raised here.

Conclusion

(fig. 132)
29 MOUNTJOY SQUARE EAST
(c.1790-1810)

Although it has lost much historic fabric, the architectural integrity of the square has been re-established. The quality of the exteriors hints at the outstanding neoclassical plasterwork inside.

The complex history of the north city is ingrained in its streets, squares and riverside, where remnants of its layered past are interwoven with contemporary interventions. While the Georgian streetscape dominates the plan, the origins of the urban pattern are derived from the lands of St Mary's Abbey. Subsequent developments in the Jervis, Moore and Gardiner estates were overlaid with a social infrastructure of churches and institutions in the nineteenth century. Urban order was fragmented in the twentieth century, an unsettled period of poverty, combined with political upheaval and expansion, that witnessed the expression of a new national identity, but also a considerable loss of historic fabric. The north city has, however, displayed resilience in the face of this profound turmoil, retaining an elegant street network and an abundance of architectural treasures.

The character of the north city is inherent in the staggered red brick terraces, stately granite façades and calp limestone churches, but also in the formally designed streetscapes that have evolved over time. Despite the loss of fabric, and reconstruction in the latter half of the twentieth century, Mountjoy Square remains a pivotal plan unit. The square retains its essential architectural integrity, and enshrined in its recent designation as an Architectural Conservation Area is an aspiration to regenerate the associated streets and laneways that were fundamental to its original composition *(fig. 132)*. Considerable conservation work has been carried out on the houses of Henrietta Street, many of which suffered neglect and the Henrietta Street Conservation Plan outlines policies and measures for implementation, providing a template for comparable works elsewhere in the city *(fig. 133)*. This street has recently hosted numerous cultural and educational events, cultivating a public awareness of its exceptional architectural legacy.

In recent years, the focus has shifted from formulaic and self-referential block insertions, towards a more stitched approach to urban repair. Successful urban interventions have the possibility to fundamentally alter our perception of the cityscape, celebrating the qualities of the existing built heritage, while introducing contemporary elements. A renewed effort to promote 'living in the city' has seen an emphasis on the re-use of vacant buildings and plots across the north city, McCullough Mulvin's conversion of the former Free Church to house a Travellers' centre being one such example. An enlightened proposal to create a cultural quarter on Parnell Square, led by Grafton Architects and Shaffrey Associates, will see the former Coláiste Mhuire school buildings adapted to house the new City Library, while restoring several town houses on the square.

(fig. 133)
14 HENRIETTA STREET
(c.1750)

This house is to be developed as a centre for the exposition of tenement life in north inner city Dublin.

(fig. 134)
DIT
GRANGEGORMAN
CAMPUS
Grangegorman Lower

The Dublin Institute
of Technology is
redeveloping the
grounds of the
historic St Brendan's
Hospital as its new
campus.

This cultural quarter, also comprising the Dublin City Gallery (The Hugh Lane), the Dublin Writers Museum and the Gate Theatre, is centred on the former eighteenth-century pleasure gardens in Parnell Square, prompting debate as to how this former amenity might be sensitively reclaimed. Proposed works to the City Fruit & Vegetable Market will see the creation of an extensive food market that will contribute to the regeneration of the surrounding streets. Further west, the Dublin Institute of Technology is to be collectively housed on the lands of Grangegorman, with existing buildings integrated into a cohesive site strategy *(fig. 134)*. As the centenary of the Easter Rising approaches, four buildings on Moore Street, including the final headquarters of the Provisional Government, are to be restored as a commemorative centre *(fig. 135)*. The Phoenix Park Conservation Management Plan prescribes an architectural survey and restoration of the gate lodges, and outlines plans to restore the Magazine Fort. Conservation work to Farmleigh House and gardens has transformed the estate into a cherished public amenity at the edge of the park.

(fig. 135)
14-17 MOORE
STREET
(c.1760)

The last surviving
original houses on the
street, including
no. 16, the final

headquarters of the
1916 Provisional
Government and a
National Monument
since 2007. The
houses are to be
restored as a
commemorative
centre.

(fig. 136)
34 MARTIN'S ROW
Chapelizod
(c.1740)

The village of Chapelizod, with medieval origins, has many historic buildings. This house, childhood home of the writer Joseph Sheridan Le Fanu (1814-73), was the setting for his well-known *The House by the Churchyard* (1863), a Gothic novel that also inspired James Joyce's *Finnegan's Wake*.

The north city is steeped in literary associations, from James Joyce to Seán O'Casey, that serve as a context in which to read and interpret its built heritage *(fig. 136)*. In 2010, Dublin was designated the fourth UNESCO City of Literature, bringing with it an international focus. The inclusion of 'The Historic City of Dublin' on the UNESCO World Heritage Tentative List in 2010 serves as an incentive to identify and celebrate the unique architectural and cultural qualities of our capital city.

The work of the National Inventory of Architectural Heritage in surveying the architectural heritage of the north city is critical in this regard, as are the various studies carried out by the Dublin Civic Trust and Dublin City Council. It is hoped that this research will serve to inform contemporary architectural endeavours, allowing the north city to evolve as part of a vibrant living capital, while its architecture continues to delight.

Further Reading

Brady, Joseph & Simms, Anngret (eds.)
Dublin through Space & Time
(Dublin, 2001)

Casey, Christine
Dublin
(New Haven & London, 2005)

Casey, Christine (ed.)
The Eighteenth-Century Dublin Town House
(Dublin, 2010)

Clarke, H.B.
Irish Historic Town Atlas, Dublin Part I, to 1610
(Dublin, 2002)

Corlett, Christiaan
Darkest Dublin
(Dublin 2008)

Craig, Maurice
Dublin 1660-1860
(London, 1952)

Cullen, Frank
Dublin 1847
(Dublin, 2015)

Curran, C.P.
Dublin Decorative Plasterwork of the 17th & 18th centuries
(London, 1967)

Daly, Mary E
Dublin, The Deposed Capital
(Cork, 1985)

De Courcy, J.W.
The Liffey in Dublin
(Dublin 1996)

Dublin City Council
The Georgian Squares of Dublin
(Dublin 2006)

Fraser, Murray
John Bull's Other Homes
(Liverpool, 1986)

Goodbody, Rob
Irish Historic Town Atlas, Dublin Part III, 1756 to 1847
(Dublin, 2014)

Lennon, Colm
Irish Historic Town Atlas, Dublin Part II, 1610 to 1756
(Dublin, 2008)

Lennon, Colm & Montague, John
John Rocque's Dublin
(Dublin, 2010)

Lucey, Conor
The Stapleton Collection
(Tralee, 2007)

McCullen, John
An Illustrated History of the Phoenix Park
(Dublin, 2009)

McCullough, Niall
Dublin: An Urban History
(Dublin, 2007)

McManus, Ruth
Dublin 1910-1940. Shaping the City & Suburbs
(Dublin, 2002)

McParland, Edward
James Gandon: Vitruvius Hibernicus
(London, 1985)

McParland, Edward
Public Architecture in Ireland 1680-1760
(New Haven & London, 2001)

McParland, Edward
The Wide Streets Commissioners
(Irish Georgian Society Bulletin, XV, no.1, 1972)

Maxwell, Constantia
Dublin under the Georges 1714-1830
(Dublin 1997)

O'Brien, Gillian & O'Kane, Finola (eds.)
Georgian Dublin
(Dublin, 2008)

O'Brien, Gillian & O'Kane, Finola (eds.)
Portrait of the City
(Dublin, 2012)

O'Neill, Michael
Bank Architecture in Dublin
(Dublin, 2011)

Pearson, Peter
The Heart of Dublin
(Dublin, 2000)

Rothery, Sean
Ireland & the New Architecture 1900-1940
(Dublin, 1991)

Web resource
Rowan, Ann Martha
www.dia.ie
Dictionary of Irish Architects 1720-1940

Registration Numbers

The structures mentioned in the text are listed below. Further information on each structure may be found on the website: www.buildingsofireland.ie and searching by the Registration Number. The structures below are listed by page number. Please note that most of the structures included in this book are privately owned and are not open to the public. However, structures marked with an asterisk (*) which include public buildings, museums, churches, railway stations and commercial properties are normally accessible

121	Clerys Department Store 18-27 O'Connell Street Lwr Reg. 50010520	130	Busáras* Store Street Reg. 50010126
122	Gresham Hotel* 20-22 O'Connell Street Upr Reg. 50010549	131	Garden of Remembrance* Parnell Square Reg. 50010658
122	Hammam Buildings 11A-13 O'Connell Street Upr Reg. 50010545	132	Abbey Theatre* Marlborough Street Not included in survey
123	Ulster Bank* 3-4 O'Connell Street Lwr Reg. 50010511	132	Liberty Hall Eden Quay Reg. 50010302
123	Post box Marlborough Street Reg. 50010238	133	AXA Insurance Co.* Wolfe Tone Street Reg. 50060519
123	Post box O'Connell Street Upr Reg. 50010555	134	Juvenile Court Smithfield Not included in survey
124	Independent House 87-90 Middle Abbey Street Reg. 50010401	134	Former Presbyterian Church 2-3 Ormond Quay Upr Reg. 50070293
125	St Thomas's Church* Cathal Brugha Street Reg. 50010237	135	The Roberts House* Dublin Zoo Reg. 50060068
125	College of Catering Cathal Brugha Street Reg. 50010236	136	29 Mountjoy Square East Reg. 50011041
126	St Fintan Road, Cabra Not included in survey	137	14 Henrietta Street Reg. 50010675
126	Chancery House Chancery Place Reg. 50070271	138	DIT Grangegorman Grangegorman Lower Reg. 50070360
127	Henrietta House Henrietta Place Reg. 50011175	138	14-17 Moore Street Reg. 50010489-92
127	Phibsborough Library* North Circular Road Reg. 50060231	139	34 Martin's Row Chapelizod Reg. 50060308
128	Mount Carmel School King's Inns Street Reg. 50060484	143	Ha'Penny Bridge Café 14 Bachelor's Walk Reg. 50010331
128	St Laurence O'Toole CBS Seville Place Reg. 50010033	144	The Flowing Tide 9 Lower Abbey Street Reg. 50010270
129	R&H Hall Alexandra Road Reg. 50060589		
129	Hendrons Dominick Street Upr Reg. 50070389		

HA'PENNY BRIDGE CAFÉ
14 Bachelor's Walk

Acknowledgements

Heritage Policy and Architectural Protection
Principal Advisor: Martin Colreavy

NIAH

Senior Architectural Advisor: William Cumming
Architectural Heritage Officers: Mildred Dunne,
TJ O'Meara, Barry O'Reilly, Jane Wales
GIS/IT: Deborah Lawlor, Cian O'Connor, T.J. O'Meara
Other NIAH Staff: Damian Murphy
Admin support: Kate Carmody, Margaret Doolan, John
Knightly, Joan Maher, Suzanne Nally, Louise Purcell
Colin Toomey, Aileen Murphy, Eddie Arthurs

Book

Author Merlo Kelly
Editors Barry O'Reilly, William Cumming
Photographer Stephen Farrell
Designed by 2B-Creative
Printed by W&G Baird

*The NIAH would like to thank all those who allowed
access to their property for the purposes of the Dublin
North City Architectural Survey and photography.*

Survey Fieldwork: Irish Architectural Surveys (Eilíse
McGuane, Edel Barry, Laura Bowen, Rosaleen Crushell,
Stephen Farrell, Sunni Goodison, Merlo Kelly, Deirdre
McDermott, Karin O'Flanagan, Jane O'Halloran, Maria
Elena Turk, Daniel Yates); Built Heritage Collective (Eilíse
McGuane, Edel Barry, Rosaleen Crushell, Natalie de
Róiste); Alastair Coey Architects (Alastair Coey, Delia
Graham, Aislinn Collins, Stephen Farrell, Robbie Graham,
Sinéad Hughes, Sarah Kerr, Leeanne Spiers).

We wish to acknowledge the assistance of:
Andrew Bonar Law; Defence Forces; Dublin City Council;
Dublin City Library and Archive; Dublin Zoo; Embassy of
the United States; Estate of Thomas W. Murphy; Irish
Architectural Archive; John A. McCullen; Lagan Building
Solutions Ltd; Military Archives; National Gallery of
Ireland; National Library of Ireland; National Maritime
Museum, Greenwich; Office of Public Works;
Photographic Unit, DAHG; Royal Irish Academy; Royal
Society of Antiquaries of Ireland; Trinity College Dublin.

Sources of Illustrations: Original photography by
Stephen Farrell, pages 2, 6, 19 (bottom), 21 (top right),
25 (bottom left), 27 (right), 28, 29, 31, 34 (bottom left),
35 (bottom), 36 (bottom), 37 (bottom), 40 (top right),
41, 45 (middle), 62 (bottom), 63 (bottom right), 64 (top
right), 65 (bottom left), 67, 68 (bottom), 69, 72 (left), 75
(top), 78, 80 (middle), 84 (bottom right), 87, 100, 102,
103 (top), 104 (top), 106 (fig. 93), 108 (fig. 97, fig. 98
main image), 111 (bottom left), 112, 118 (bottom), 120
(right), 121 (bottom, right), 123 (left), 125 (except top
left), 129 (bottom), 130 (bottom right), 131 (top), 133.
Ownership of archival images is individually
acknowledged. Maps provided by Royal Irish Academy
from Irish Historic Town Atlas, no. 19, Dublin II, 1610 to
1756 by Colm Lennon (Dublin 2008) and Irish Historic
Town Atlas, no. 26, Dublin III, 1756 to 1847 by Rob
Goodbody (Dublin 2014). Drawing of St Mary's Abbey on
page 10 is from Dublin, One Thousand Years by Stephen
Conlin, published by The O'Brien Press Ltd, Dublin,
Stephen Conlin. All other photography is by field
recorders for the NIAH, or by NIAH staff. The NIAH has
made every effort to source and acknowledge the owners
of all of the archival illustrations included in this book.
The NIAH apologises for any omissions made and would
be happy to include acknowledgements in future issues.

Please note that the majority of the structures included
in the Dublin North City Architectural Survey are
privately owned and are not open to the public.

ISBN: 978-1-4064-2877-3

© Government of Ireland 2015

THE FLOWING TIDE
9 Lower Abbey
Street

Stained glass by
Stanley Tomlin,
1955.